VOCABULARY
FROM
CLASSICAL ROOTS

Norma Fifer   Nancy Flowers

E

Educators Publishing Service
Cambridge and Toronto

Acknowledgments

Illustrations in *Vocabulary from Classical Roots—E* have been taken from the following sources:

Catchpenny Prints. 163 Popular Engravings from the Eighteenth Century. New York: Dover Publications, Inc., 1970.

1800 Woodcuts by Thomas Bewick and His School. Blanche Cirker, ed. New York: Dover Publications, Inc., 1962.

Food and Drink. A Pictorial Archive from Nineteenth-Century Sources. Selected by Jim Harter. Third revised edition. New York: Dover Publications, Inc., 1983.

Harter's Picture Archive for Collage and Illustration. Jim Harter, ed. New York: Dover Publications, Inc., 1978.

Huber, Richard. *Treasury of Fantastic and Mythological Creatures. 1,087 Renderings from Historic Sources.* New York: Dover Publications, Inc., 1981.

Humorous Victorian Spot Illustrations. Carol Belanger Grafton, ed. New York: Dover Publications, Inc., 1985.

The Illustrator's Handbook. Compiled by Harold H. Hart. New York: Galahad Books, 1978.

Lively Advertising Cuts of the Twenties and Thirties. 1,102 Illustrations of Animals, Food and Dining, Children, etc. Leslie Cabarga and Marcie McKinnon, eds. New York: Dover Publications, Inc., 1990.

Men. A Pictorial Archive from Nineteenth-Century Sources. Selected by Jim Harter. New York: Dover Publications, Inc., 1980.

More Silhouettes. 868 Copyright-Free Illustrations for Artists and Craftsmen. Carol Belanger Grafton, ed. New York: Dover Publications, Inc., 1982.

Old-Fashioned Silhouettes. 942 Copyright-Free Illustrations. Carol Belanger Grafton, ed. New York: Dover Publications, Inc., 1993.

1,001 Advertising Cuts from the Twenties and Thirties. Compiled and arranged by Leslie Cabarga, Richard Greene, and Marina Cruz. New York: Dover Publications, Inc, 1987.

Silhouettes. A Pictorial Archive of Varied Illustrations. Carol Belanger Grafton, ed. New York: Dover Publications, Inc., 1979.

3,800 Early Advertising Cuts. Selected and arranged by Carol Belanger Grafton. New York: Dover Publications, Inc., 1991.

2001 Decorative Cuts and Ornaments. Carol Belanger Grafton, ed. New York: Dover Publications, Inc., 1988.

Victorian Spot Illustrations, Alphabets and Ornaments from Porret's Type Catalog. Carol Belanger Grafton, ed. New York: Dover Publications, Inc., 1982.

Women. A Pictorial Archive from Nineteenth-Century Sources. Selected by Jim Harter. Second revised edition. New York: Dover Publications, Inc., 1982.

Cover photograph by Katharine Klubock

Printed in U.S.A.
ISBN 0-8388-2260-6

1 2 3 4 5 VHG 08 07 06 05 04

Contents

Preface

Vocabulary from Classical Roots encourages you to look at words as members of families in the way astronomers see stars as parts of constellations. Here you will become acquainted with constellations of words descended from Greek and Latin, visible in families that cluster around such subjects as government, business, the military, and law.

This book can do more than increase your recognition of words; perhaps it will encourage you to study Latin or Greek. More immediately, though, it can remind you that English is a metaphorical language. By returning to the origins of English words you will move closer to knowing how language began: in naming people, things, and concrete actions. So enjoy recognizing the classical heritage of both familiar and unusual words.

Notes on Using *Vocabulary from Classical Roots*

1. **Latin (L.) and Greek (G.) forms.** Complete sets of these forms help to explain the spelling of their English derivatives. Practice pronouncing these words by following some simple rules.

   To pronounce Latin:
   > Every *a* sounds like *ah,* as in *swan.*
   > The letter *v* is pronounced like *w.*
   > The letter *e* at the end of a word, as in the verb *amare,* should sound like the *e* in *egg.*

   To pronounce Greek:
   > As in Latin, *a* sounds like *ah.*
   > The diphthong *ei* rhymes with *say;* for example, the verb *agein* rhymes with *rain.*
   > *Au,* as in *autos,* sounds like the *ow* in *owl,* and *os* rhymes with *gross.*

2. **Diacritical marks.** Following every defined word in *Vocabulary from Classical Roots* is the guide to pronunciation, as in (dī ə krĭt′ ĭ kəl). The letter that looks like an upside-down *e* (called a *schwa*) is pronounced like the *a* in *about.* You will find a key to the diacritical marks used in this book on the inside front cover.

3. **Derivation.** Information in brackets after the guide to pronunciation for a word gives further information about the source of that word. For example, after **diacritical** (dī ə krĭt′ ĭ kəl), under *dia* <G. "apart," would appear [*krinein* <G. "to separate"]. Thus, the word *diacritical* is made up of two words that come from Greek and means "separating the parts" and, consequently, "distinguishing."

4. **Familiar Words and Challenge Words.** Listed next to groups of defined words may be one or two sets of words belonging to the same family. You probably already know the Familiar Words in the shaded boxes. Try to figure out the meanings of the Challenge Words, and if you are curious, look them up in a dictionary.

5. **Nota Bene.** *Nota bene* means "note well" and is usually abbreviated to *N.B.* In *Vocabulary from Classical Roots,* NOTA BENE calls your attention informally to other words related to the theme of the lesson.

6. **Exercises.** The exercises help you determine how well you have learned the words in each lesson while also serving as practice for examinations such as the SAT: synonyms and antonyms, analogies, words in context, and sentence completions. Further exercises illustrate words used in sentences, test recognition of roots, and offer writing practice.

LESSONS 1 AND 2

Here and There

Directions

1. Each KEY word is listed under a Greek or Latin root. Try to determine how the KEY word and the Familiar Words listed in the margin relate to the meaning of the root.
2. Determine the pronunciation of each KEY word and say it aloud. Refer to the inside front cover for a guide to the diacritical marks.
3. Learn the definition(s) of each KEY word. Observe how the word is used in the sample sentence(s). Notice that some words have both a concrete and a metaphorical use.
4. Notice whether the KEY word is used as another part of speech or if it has an antonym.
5. Add to your understanding of the KEY words by observing all the additional information: the Latin epigraphs (phrases at the beginning of each lesson), the Challenge Words, and the Nota Bene references.
6. Practice using the words by completing the exercises.

LESSON 1

Requiescat in pace.
May he or she rest in peace.*

Key Words		
abstruse	interpolate	propinquity
acquiesce	interpose	quiescent
extrude	interregnum	rapprochement
interloper	juxtapose	requiem
internecine	obtrude	unrequited

*The initials *R.I.P.* sometimes appear on gravestones.

Familiar Words
intercept
interdict
interest
interfere
interim
interject
interlude
intermediary
intermission
intermural
international
intersperse
intervene

Challenge Words
intercede
interfuse
interlocutor
intermezzo
internuncio

INTER <L. "between"

1. **interloper** (ĭn´ tər lōp´ ər) [*looper* <Dutch "runner"]
n. One who intrudes by meddling or trespassing on the rights of others.

Mrs. Proudie, the bishop's wife, is such an officious **interloper** in church matters that people sarcastically refer to her as "the Bishop of Barchester."

interlope, *v.*

2. **internecine** (ĭn tər nē´ sēn, ĭn tər nēs´ ən, ĭn tər nĕs´ ēn, ĭn tər nē´ sīn) [*necare* <L. "to slay"]
adj. 1. Very destructive to both sides in a conflict; involving slaughter and carnage.

The **internecine** cost of the victory of King Pyrrhus of Epirus over the Romans in 279 B.C. is remembered today in the phrase "Pyrrhic victory."

2. Pertaining to struggle or conflict within a group, organization, or nation.

The **internecine** struggle of the American Civil War left the country devastated.

3. **interpolate** (ĭn tûr´ pə lāt´) [*polire* <L. "to polish"]
tr. v. 1. To insert or add something between other parts, especially in a text or written work.

For the music lesson scene in *The Barber of Seville*, the composer, Gioacchino Rossini, let every singer in the role of Rosina **interpolate** an aria of her choice.

2. To introduce material that severely alters a text or falsifies it.

Eighteenth-century acting companies freely **interpolated** new speeches, scenes, or denouements into plays they were performing, even works by Shakespeare.

interpolation, *n.*; **interpolative**, *adj.*

4. **interregnum** (ĭn´ tər rĕg´ nəm) [*regnum* <L. "reign"]
n. 1. Any period of time when a state is without a ruler or has a provisional government, especially between the reign of a sovereign and a successor.

During the **interregnum** of 1649 to 1660, Oliver Cromwell and his Roundheads controlled the English government.

2. An interval between controlling elements; an interruption in an otherwise continuous function or process.

"The old is dying and the new cannot be born; in this **interregnum** there arises a great diversity of morbid symptoms."—Antonio Gramsci

Familiar Words
component
composer
dispose
expose
expound
impostor
opponent
pose
positive
postpone
proponent
proposition
purpose
suppose
transpose

PONO, PONERE, POSUI, POSITUM
<L. "to put," "to place"

5. **interpose** (ĭn tər pōz´) [*inter* <L. "between"] *tr. v.* and *intr. v.* 1. To insert between parts of something; to interject in a conversation.

The correction of the Julian calendar authorized by Pope Gregory XIII in 1582 eliminated ten days and **interposed** an extra day every four years.

2. To apply pressure or influence; to meddle; to interfere.

When the vicar's bride arrives in Hatfield, she **interposes** herself as the arranger of entertainments, usurping the role that Emma Woodhouse has hitherto claimed as hers.

interposition, *n.*

Challenge Words
apposite
deposition
poseur
posit
supposititious

6. **juxtapose** (jŭk stə pōz´) [*juxta* <L. "close together"] *tr. v.* To place side by side.

In the poem "Pied Beauty," Gerard Manley Hopkins **juxtaposes** contrasting words—"swift, slow; sweet, sour; adazzle, dim"—to illustrate the marvel of the world's diverse forms and textures.

juxtaposition, *n.*

Familiar Words
approach
approximate
irreproachable
proximity
reproach

PROPE <L. "near"
PROPINQUUS <L. "near"

7. **propinquity** (prō pĭng´ kwə tē) [*pro* <L. "forth"] *n.* 1. Nearness; proximity.

Propinquity
is the province of cats. Living by accident, . . .
cats take their chances, love by need or nearness
as long as the need lasts, as long as the nearness
is near enough.—Alastair Reid

2. Kinship.

Although the tempestuous relationship of Catherine Earnshaw and Heathcliff is unfulfilled, it leads to the uneasy **propinquity** through marriage of her daughter and his son.

8. **rapprochement** (rȧ prôsh mäN′) [*ap* = *ad* <L. "to," "toward"]
n. Reconciliation; restoration of cordial
relations, especially between two countries.

After many centuries of conflict, the **rapprochement** of Israel and the Vatican occurred when formal relations were established in 1993.

QUIES, QUIETIS <L. "quiet," "rest"
QUIESCO, QUIESCERE, QUIEVI, QUIETUM <L. "to rest,"
"to remain quiet"

Familiar Words
acquit
coy
quiet
quit
tranquil

Challenge Words
disquietude
inquietude
quietism

9. **quiescent** (kwī ĕs′ ənt, kwē ĕs′ ənt)
adj. At rest; dormant; motionless.

Family members' emotions in China in the 1960s
may have appeared **quiescent**, but Ting Ling
describes conflicts churning beneath the calm exteriors.

quiescence, *n.*

10. **acquiesce** (ăk′ wē ĕs′) [*ac* = *ad* <L. "to," "toward"]
intr. v. To agree or consent without any objection.

"If the changes that we fear [in language] be thus irresistible, what remains to **acquiesce** with silence. . .?"—Samuel Johnson, Preface to *A Dictionary of the English Language*

acquiescence, *n.*; **acquiescent**, *adj.*

11. **requiem** (rĕk′ wē əm, rē′ kwē əm) [*re* <L. "back," "again"]
n. A mass or service for the repose of departed souls; music, poetry, or other composition for the dead.

Hamlet learns of Ophelia's suicide when he hears the priest say, "We should profane the service of the dead, / To sing a **requiem**, and such rest to her / As to peace-parted souls."

12. **unrequited** (ŭn′ rĭ kwīt′ əd) [*un* <Germanic "not"]
adj. Not reciprocal; not given in payment or returned in kind.

In Arthurian legend, Elaine dies of a broken heart because of her **unrequited** love for Lancelot, who is devoted to Queen Guinevere.

unrequitable, *adj.*
Antonym: **requited**

NOTA BENE: Although frequently used, the word *unrequited* does not appear in most dictionaries; the meaning of the negative *un* form is implied. The word usually appears in the context of a one-sided love relationship. However, *unrequited* can also mean "not avenged; without retaliation for a wrong or injury"; for example, Christian teaching advises letting a wrong go *unrequited* by "turning the other cheek." *Requite* rarely turns up in contemporary speech, but one might say that polite guests *requite* their host's hospitality with a thoughtful gift.

Familiar Words
intrude
protrude

Challenge Word
detrude

TRUDO, TRUDERE, TRUSI, TRUSUM <L. "to push"]

13. **abstruse** (ăb strōōs′) [*ab* <L. "away from"]
adj. Difficult to understand; complex.

Without some background in physics, an audience would find a lecture on thermodynamics and entropy **abstruse**.

abstruseness, *n.*

14. **extrude** (ĭk strōōd′) [*ex* <L. "from," "out of"]
tr. v. To push or thrust out a liquid or malleable substance that retains or solidifies into a predetermined shape.

The chambered nautilus **extrudes** a nacreous substance that hardens into a shell of progressively larger chambers to accommodate the animal's growth.

extrusion, *n.*

15. **obtrude** (ŏb trōōd′) [*ob* <L. "off," "against"]
tr. v. and *intr. v.* 1. To force one's ideas or oneself insistently upon others.

Pretending to be humble, Uriah Heep **obtrudes** in the business affairs of the Wickfields until David Copperfield's friends come to the rescue.

2. To thrust or push out; to protrude noticeably, often in an undesirable way.

During years when the water level of Mono Lake in California dropped, *tufas*, irregular knobbed and spired formations of calcium carbonate, began to **obtrude** above the surface.

obtruder, *n.*; **obtrusive**, *adj.*; **obtrusiveness**, *n.*; **obtrusion**, *n.*

EXERCISE 1A  Circle the letter of the best SYNONYM for the word in bold-faced type.

1. A prolonged **interregnum**   a. conspiracy   b. continued reign
   c. break in continuity   d. king's stand-in   e. questioning
2. **abstruse** arguments   a. clear   b. confusing   c. verbose
   d. important   e. brief
3. **acquiescence** to the contract   a. indifference   b. objection
   c. reaction   d. attention   e. agreement
4. arrival of a(n) **interloper**   a. impostor   b. jogger   c. intruder
   d. reporter   e. interpreter
5. **extruded** into a plastic mold   a. filtered   b. leaked   c. heated
   d. pressed   e. blown
6. to distort by **interpolation**   a. interpretation   b. insertion
   c. misreading   d. mediation   e. elimination
7. **rapprochement** at the peace talks   a. acquiescence   b. discussion
   c. hostility   d. reconciliation   e. neighborliness
8. to **interpose** an irrelevant question   a. obtrude   b. extrude
   c. interject   d. withdraw   e. dispute
9. the **propinquity** of Minneapolis and St. Paul   a. remoteness
   b. nearness   c. kinship   d. separateness   e. property laws

Circle the letter of the best ANTONYM for the word in bold-faced type.

10. to **juxtapose** contrasting colors   a. separate   b. project
    c. alternate   d. relocate   e. join
11. **obtrusive** freeway billboards   a. unnecessary   b. garish
    c. inconspicuous   d. annoying   e. excessive
12. a period of **quiescence**   a. boredom   b. rapprochement
    c. sleep   d. animosity   e. agitation
13. **unrequited** affections   a. timeless   b. spurned   c. reciprocated
    d. tolerated   e. unavenged

EXERCISE 1B   Circle the letter of the sentence in which the word in bold-faced type is used incorrectly.

1. a. The death of the Italian poet Alessandro Manzoni in 1873 stirred
      Guiseppe Verdi to complete his unfinished **Requiem**.
   b. After years of feuding, the reunion brought the family together
      in conviviality and **requiem**.
   c. The **requiem** mass for earthquake victims took place at the parish
      church.
   d. Yevgeny Yevtushenko's poem "Babi Yar" serves as a **requiem**
      mourning the massacre of 35,000 Ukrainian Jews outside Kiev.

2. a. Although high tides during winter storms were a continuing threat, the beach cottage was appealing precisely because of its **propinquity** to the sea.

b. Accompanying her husband on the Lewis and Clark expedition to the West Coast, Sacajawea used her **propinquity** to the Shoshone people to secure safe passage through their territory.

c. Two important figures in Central American mythology—Quetzalcoatl, the plumed serpent god, and Topiltzin, the last king of the Toltecs—share an unlikely **propinquity**, even a single identity.

d. In the 1950s Amy Vanderbilt's book on etiquette, **propinquity**, and good manners was a best-seller.

3. a. Because circumstances prevented the college of cardinals from electing a pope, a papal **interregnum** lasted from 1268 to 1271.

b. Innovations by four revolutionary governments significantly changed French politics during the **interregnum** between the execution of King Louis XVI in 1793 and the restoration of the monarchy with Louis XVIII in 1815.

c. Many parents plan an **interregnum** in their professional careers while their children are young.

d. Travelers often wait for airlines to offer bargain **interregnums** before planning holiday vacations.

4. a. Family members in Louise Erdrich's novel *Tracks* keep **internecine** rivalry alive through trickery, thievery, and mayhem.

b. **Internecine** dissension developed within Japanese shogunates as military factions vied for power with imperial court factions.

c. Festivals featuring **internecine** traditions maintain harmony among ethnic groups throughout America.

d. Huck Finn sees no logic in the **internecine** feuding that leads to the death of his friend Buck.

5. a. Now a revered landmark, the Eiffel Tower was once viewed as an **obtrusive** eyesore.

b. Some cities are in crisis because garbage dumps are **obtruding** too fast and too expansively.

c. Scavengers searching for sunken ships and their rich cargoes **obtrude** divers to explore wreckage on the ocean floor.

d. Environmentalists fear that the **obtrusion** of off-road vehicles driven recklessly through forests and deserts may permanently damage plant and animal life.

6. a. Composed of diverse images from her reading and experience, Marianne Moore's poetry has the quality of a verbal collage that sometimes makes it difficult to **interpolate**.

b. After completion of his autobiographical poem *The Prelude*, William Wordsworth made many revisions and **interpolated** thirty-two lines honoring the British statesman Edmund Burke.

    c. The 1976 copyright law prohibits the **interpolation** of any words in a dramatic performance without the author's permission.

    d. When students' papers depend too heavily on unsupported generalizations, teachers are likely to recommend that the writers **interpolate** specific examples to defend their ideas.

EXERCISE 1C

Fill in each blank with the most appropriate word from Lesson 1. Use a word or any of its forms only once.

1. When construction of a hydroelectric plant threatened to make a variety of snapdragon extinct, Kate Furbish, a botanist,

    _____ successfully to save the endangered flower.

2. Sir Walter Scott concludes his novel *The Talisman* with the

    _____ of two natural enemies when the Christian Crusader Richard Lionheart acknowledges that the code he follows is less honorable than that of the Muslim Saracen Saladin.

3. _____ persecution and genocide have decimated Cambodia.

4. A recent exhibition of seventeenth-century Dutch painters

    _____ portraits of a husband and wife whose likenesses had hung in separate museums for more than one hundred years.

5. Ibsen introduces conflict in *The Master Builder* with the sudden

    arrival of Hilda Wangel, a(n) _____ who stirs old passions and domestic unrest.

6. The pastry cook's hand held steady as the pastry tube

    _____ an even rope of frosting.

7. Refusing to _____ to pressure from the white community, Autherine Lucy enrolled in 1956 at the University of Alabama, but threats and rioting forced her departure and expulsion a few days later.

8. Rod Serling's film _____ *for a Heavyweight* portrays the decline of a prizefighter who cannot accept the end of his days in the ring.

9. During their _____ months of winter sleep, polar bears recycle their body products, emerging thinner but strong and healthy, with no deterioration of bone.

10. Because of James Joyce's invented words, playful grammatical forms, parodies, riddles, and obscure allusions, many readers find his novels _____.

11. In *A MidSummer Night's Dream*, Oberon notices Helena's _____ love for Demetrius and sends his assistant Puck to correct the situation by placing a few magical drops in Demetrius's eyes, but Puck treats the wrong person.

EXERCISE 1D

Replace the word or phrase in italics with a key word (or any of its forms) from Lesson 1.

Before the outbreak of the Russian Revolution in 1917, political unrest was intense for several reasons. One was the (1) *existence side by side* of an impotent working class and an insensitive autocracy. Czarina Alexandra, wife of Czar Nicholas II, (2) *exerted forcible influence* in governmental affairs, often reproaching her husband for weakness; both depended upon the (3) *intruder* Rasputin, whom many believed to be not only (4) *insistently meddling*, but also corrupt. Other reasons for discontent were severe war losses, food shortages, the Czar's harsh response to a workers' strike, and the arbitrary dismissal of the legislative body, the Duma.

Refusing to be (5) *silent*, however, the Duma appointed a provisional government that forced Czar Nicholas to (6) *consent without objection* to abdication. The (7) *interruption in leadership* that followed brought months of (8) *fierce internal* struggle among the three main factions. A brief government headed by Aleksandr Kerenski was driven into an unsatisfactory (9) *reconciliation* with opponents, but in November 1917 Vladimir Lenin headed a new Bolshevik cabinet. At his direction members of the royal family were held captive following the Czar's abdication and were executed in 1918.

1. _____   6. _____
2. _____   7. _____
3. _____   8. _____
4. _____   9. _____
5. _____

LESSON 2

Alter idem.
The same as oneself.—CICERO

Key Words		
altercation	epitaph	paradox
altruism	epithet	paragon
anathema	epitome	parameter
antithesis	eponymous	peripatetic
ephemeral	paradigm	peripheral

Familiar Words
alter
alteration
alternative

Challenge Words
alter ego
subaltern

ALTER <L. "other"

1. **altercation** (ôl′ tər kā′ shən)
   [*altercari* <L. "to have difference with another"]
   n. A noisy quarrel.

   In the British Parliament of the 1880s **altercations** over Home Rule for Ireland arose frequently between the prime minister William Gladstone and the Irish member Charles Parnell.

   altercate, *v.*

2. **altruism** (ăl′ trōō ĭz′ əm)
   n. Concern for the welfare of others; unselfishness.

   The economist Barbara Ward asserts that both individuals and governments prosper when sagacious **altruism** governs their cooperation.

   altruistic, *adj.*

Familiar Words
epicenter
epidemic
epidermis
epiglottis
epigram
epigraph
epilepsy
epilogue
epiphany
epoch
episode

EPI <G. "on," "toward"

3. **ephemeral** (ĭ fĕm′ ər əl)   [*hemera* <G. "day"]
   adj. Lasting for a very short time (literally, for one day); transitory; not everlasting.

   The experiment in harmonious community living begun in 1841 at Brook Farm proved to be **ephemeral,** lasting only until 1847 despite the hopes of its members to share intellectual stimulation and manual labor.

   ephemera, *n.* (plural)

Challenge Words
epicycle
epidural
episcopal
episcope
epistemology
epistrophe
epitasis
epithesis
epithet

4. **epitaph** (ĕp′ ə tăf′) [*taphos* <G. "tomb"] *n.* An inscription on a tombstone in memory of the person buried there; a brief (literary) summary of a dead person's life.

Jane Austen's **epitaph** in Winchester Cathedral attests to "the benevolence of her heart."

5. **epitome** (ĭ pĭt′ ə mē) [*temnein* <G. "to cut"] *n.* A typical representation of something; a person who embodies a quality.

"A man so various that he seem'd to be / Not one, but all mankind's **epitome**."—John Dryden

epitomize, *v.*

6. **eponymous** (ĭ pŏn′ ə məs) [*onym* = *onoma* <G. "name"] *adj.* Referring to the name of a person, a mythical being, or a literary figure associated with something, or to a word incorporating the name of such a person (as in *braille, cardigan, silhouette, sandwich,* and *spoonerism*).

An arbiter of fashion in the court of Louis XV the **eponymous** Marquise de Pompadour wore her hair upswept from the forehead in the style that became known as the pompadour.

eponym, *n.*; **eponymy**, *n.*

NOTA BENE: Although *epicurean* begins with *epi*, its source is the eponymous Greek philosopher Epicurus, who is sometimes interpreted as endorsing self-indulgence: an *epicure* is someone of refined taste in food and drink. However, Epicurus believed that happiness comes from moderation. He advocated rational thought and self-control as a means of heightening pleasure and avoiding pain.

PARA <G. "beside"

7. **paradigm** (păr′ ə dīm′, păr′ ə dĭm′) [*deiknunai* <G. "to show"] *n.* An example serving to illustrate a process, pattern, or concept.

For many centuries theater design has followed the Greek **paradigm** of a proscenium with exits at the right and left of a rectangular stage.

Familiar Words
parable
parabola
paragraph
parallel
parallelogram
paralysis
paramecium
paranoid
paraphernalia
paraphrase
paraplegia
parasite

Challenge Words
paragenesis
parallax
parallelepiped
paralogism
paramnesia
parataxis

8. **paradox** (păr′ ə dŏks′)
[*doxa* <G. "opinion," "judgment"]
n. A statement that seems contradictory but contains a truth or valid deduction.

"There is that glorious epicurean **paradox** uttered by my friend the historian, in one of his flashing moments; 'Give us the luxuries of life, and we will dispense with its necessaries.'"—Oliver Wendell Holmes

paradoxical, *adj.*

9. **paragon** (păr′ ə gŏn′, păr′ ə gən) [*akonan* <G. "to sharpen"]
n. A model of excellence or perfection.

Aspasia became known in Athens as a **paragon** of oratory, inspiring Plato, Socrates, and Pericles with her eloquence and skill in composing speeches.

NOTA BENE: The definitions of *epitome*, *paradigm*, and *paragon* overlap somewhat. Note than an *epitome* is a general representation of something, not necessarily good or admirable. One person may be the epitome of courage and another the epitome of cowardice; a room may be the epitome of tastelessness or of classical grandeur. A *paradigm* provides a basic form of something whose process, pattern, or concept can serve as a model, as in automobile assembly, the conjugation of verbs, or the working of an algebra problem. A *paragon*, usually a person, is someone outstanding for some personal quality or remarkable achievement.

10. **parameter** (pə răm′ ə tər) [*metron* <G. "measure"]
n. 1. In mathematics, a constant that has variable values and is used to determine other variables.

If a gorilla were scaled up to the size of King Kong, the **parameters** of its volume and cross-sectional area show that the creature would collapse under its own weight.

2. A factor that determines a range of variations; a boundary.

One of the functions of the Occupational Safety and Health Administration is to set **parameters** for the workplace, such as humane schedules and physical safeguards.

Familiar Words
paradise
perigee
perimeter
period
periodical
periscope

Challenge Words
pericardium
pericycle
perihelion
periodontal
periphrastic
peripteral
peristalsis
peristyle
peritoneum

Familiar Words
hypothesis
parenthesis
synthesize
theme
thesaurus
treasure

parametric, *adj.*

PERI <G. "around"

11.　**peripatetic**　(pĕr´ ə pə tĕt′ ĭk)
　　[*patein* <G. "to walk"]
　　adj. Walking or traveling about.

At age nineteen the English author Laurie Lee made a **peripatetic** journey across Spain, walking from village to village and playing his violin in cafes for meals and lodging.

12.　**peripheral**　(pə rĭf′ ər əl)　[*pherein* <G. "to carry"]
　　adj. 1. Pertaining to the boundary of an area.

When the Romans invaded Britain, they built camps whose **peripheral** walls still surround central sections of many English cities.

2. Of minor importance.

Gloria Steinem called attention to the fact that the thirteen qualified women astronauts appeared to be **peripheral** because they remained unmentioned in publicity during the early years of the space program.

periphery, *n.*

NOTA BENE: A test of peripheral vision determines the capacity of the eye when focused directly ahead to see objects on the perimeter of the field, out of the corner of the eye.

TITHENAI <G. "to put"

13.　**anathema**　(ə năth′ ə mə)　[*ana* <G. "up"]
　　n. 1. A person or thing detested and shunned.

Freelance photographers known as paparazzi have become **anathema** to celebrities upon whom they obtrude.

2. A curse, especially a formal church ban or excommunication.

Pope Leo X in 1520 proclaimed an **anathema** against Martin Luther for his attack on the sale of indulgences, a practice the Pope himself had encouraged.

Challenge Words
apothecary
diathesis
metathesis
prosthesis

anathematize, *v.*; anathematic, *adj.*

14. **antithesis** (ăn tĭth′ ə sĭs) [*anti* <G. "opposite," "against"]
n. 1. An exact opposite; a complete contrast.

Ella Fitzgerald's sinuous vocal improvisations are the **antithesis** of the thunderous drive of rock music although the term *popular music* can refer to both.

2. A rhetorical form juxtaposing contrasting ideas, often in parallel structure.

Minna Antrim juxtaposes two kinds of knowledge to create **antithesis**: "To know one's self is wisdom, but to know one's neighbor is genius."

antithetical, *adj.*

NOTA BENE: History students become familiar with another meaning of *antithesis.* Karl Marx borrowed from Friedrich Hegel a theory of the historical process having three stages: thesis, antithesis, and synthesis. Envisioning a classless society, Marx perceived economic modes of production as the concern of the first stage, or thesis; internal tensions and disagreements would follow as the second stage, or antithesis; and the resolution of differences would bring the third stage, or synthesis, the completion of the cycle and the realization of the perfect socialist state.

15. **epithet** (ĕp′ ə thĕt´) [*epi* <G. "on," "toward"]
n. A word or phrase used positively or negatively that characterizes or describes a person or thing, added to or replacing a name.

The repetition of **epithets** in *The Odyssey*, such as "rosy-fingered Dawn" and "gray-eyed Athena," served as a mnemonic for the minstrel as well as for the listener.

EXERCISE 2A

Circle the letter of the best SYNONYM for the word in bold-faced type.

1. A mathematical **paradigm**   a. angle   b. hypothesis   c. model   d. parameter   e. equivalent
2. to hurl a(n) **epithet**   a. weapon   b. disparaging phrase   c. threat   d. afterthought   e. compliment
3. a(n) **paragon** among chefs   a. example of incompetence   b. epitome   c. anathema   d. example of excellence   e. example of creativity

4. to precipitate **altercations** a. alternatives b. conspiracies
   c. solutions d. antitheses e. squabbles
5. appropriate **epitaphs** a. witty sayings b. birth announcements
   c. prefatory remarks d. last words e. graveside inscriptions
6. budgetary **parameters** a. excesses b. perimeters c. calculations
   d. limits e. interregnums
7. the **epitome** of fair play a. paradigm b. parameter c. anathema
   d. embodiment e. antithesis
8. remembered **anathemas** a. ghosts b. beloved persons
   c. requiems d. despised beings e. quarrels
9. **paradoxical** situations a. contradictory b. true c. mysterious
   d. illustrative e. parallel
10. dedicated to **altruism** a. honesty b. faith c. self-interest
    d. altercation e. unselfishness
11. a familiar **eponym** a. bold action b. friendly greeting
    c. opening statement d. descriptive phrase e. name's source

Circle the letter of the best ANTONYM for the word in bold-faced type.

12. **peripheral** to the debate a. obtrusive b. essential c. immaterial
    d. ephemeral e. tangential
13. **ephemeral** a. short-lived b. eponymous c. enduring
    d. daytime e. derivative
14. a **peripatetic** ice-cream vendor a. pitiful b. traveling
    c. well-equipped d. stationary e. peripheral
15. **antithetical** political positions a. opposite b. synonymous
    c. outrageous d. well-analyzed e. courageous

EXERCISE 2B

Circle the letter of the sentence in which the word in bold-faced type is used incorrectly.

1. a. Dorothea Lange's famous photograph of a migrant mother and
      her children **epitomizes** the poverty and despair of dustbowl
      refugees during the 1930s.
   b. In the Deep South moon pies are the **epitome** of snack food,
      combining the sweetness of marshmallow cream with chocolate-
      or butterscotch-covered vanilla wafers.
   c. The **epitome** of greed, two social-climbing daughters coldly and
      persistently impoverish their doting father in Balzac's *Pere Goriot*.
   d. Mountain climbers did not reach the **epitome** of Mount Everest
      until 1953.
2. a. For Mahalia Jackson blues and gospel songs are the **antithesis** of
      one another because "Blues are the songs of despair, but gospel
      songs are the songs of hope."

    b. Some students became so **antithetical** that they refused to write the major paper required for the term.

    c. When Juliet hears that her cousin Tybalt has died at the hands of her beloved Romeo, she cries, "Beautiful tyrant! Fiend angelical!" compressing her **antithetical** feelings into the extreme paradox called oxymoron.

    d. Toni Morrison's two protagonists in *Sula* represent **antitheses** in personal style: Nel Greene is loyal to home and community, while Sula Peace is independent and rebellious.

3. a. After a scalawag cut off the tail of the donkey that Saint Thomas à Becket was riding in Kent, he uttered the memorable **anathema** that all Kentish men be born with donkeys' tails.

    b. To sinners depicted in the classical art and literature, the Furies were **anathema**: relentless avengers against wrongdoing, with heads of writhing snakes and hands bearing whips and torches.

    c. When **anathematized** by officials of the medieval Catholic church, members lost the right to be buried in sacred ground, to associate with other Christians, or to receive the sacraments of the church.

    d. A Roman medical manuscript from the sixth century pictures a pain-killing mandragora root and gives a prescription for **anathematizing** patients who are to be "cut or burnt."

EXERCISE 2C

Fill in each blank with the most appropriate word from Lesson 2. Use a word or any of its forms only once.

1. Although university students in China have pressed for social

   change, their influence has been _____ because they represent such a small percentage of the population.

2. Setting up their productions on wagons, _____ acting companies in the Middle Ages moved from town to town, performing in churches or village squares.

3. You can conjugate the six tenses of the verb *swim, swam, swum* by

   following this _____: "you lie, you lay, you will lie, you have lain, you had lain, you will have lain."

4. Charlotte Perkins Gilman sees the following situation as

   a(n) _____: "The women who do the most work get the least money, but the women who have the most money do the least work."

5. After her fiance's death in World War I, Vera Brittain recalled

   the _____ happiness of her youth in a poem that concludes, "I thought that spring must last for evermore, / For I was young and loved, and it was May."

6. While Bernarda Alba tries to restrain her five daughters, their

repressed passions and hatreds lead to _____ that end in death.

7. _____ have been bestowed on several notable figures in American history, among them Stonewall Jackson, Honest Abe Lincoln, and Boss Tweed.

8. Because the _____ of budget and technical skill affect the precision of high school students' science experiments, a ten percent margin of error is realistic.

9. Distressed by the ignorance and poverty in their French town, Bartholomea Capitanio and Vincentia Gerosa committed their lives to the _____ service of teaching the young and nursing the sick.

10. Louis Pasteur, the _____ of pasteurization, discovered the process of applying heat to kill microorganisms that cause fermentation and disease.

11. Greta Garbo, a legend in cinematic history, was not only a(n) _____ of beauty but also of instinctive response to her directors and the camera.

12. "Here lies one who meant well, tried a little, failed much: —surely that may be his _____ of which he need not be ashamed."—Robert Louis Stevenson

EXERCISE 2D   Replace the word or phrase in italics with a key word (or any of its forms) from Lesson 2.

The story of Captain Álvar Núñez Cabeza de Vaca is the (1) *complete opposite* of many historical accounts of the Spanish presence in the New World, where (2) *noisy disagreements* between the interlopers and the native peoples often ended in brutality and death. Surviving a shipwreck in 1528, Cabeza de Vaca endured six years of hardship as a slave, gaining trust, however, among the native peoples of the Southwest through prayer, healing, and practical knowledge. He became famous as a(n) (3) *excellent model* of compassion and (4) *concern for the welfare of others.*

In 1534 he joined three other escaped captives, an African slave and two Spaniards, whom he trained in his skills. The native peoples especially admired the African Estavanico for his talent in mime and translation. Traveling westward, escorted from village to village by native guides, the (5) *wandering* shamans earned the (6) *characterizing phrase* "children of the sun" because they always appeared from the east.

As they turned south into Mexico, however, they encountered a(n)

(7) *hated thing*—a Spanish slaving party—but from a sympathetic captain, Cabeza de Vaca secured a guarantee of protection for his followers. When he reached the capital city after eight years of near starvation and one thousand miles of wandering, he and his companions were honored with an official holiday and a banquet.

1. _____   5. _____

2. _____   6. _____

3. _____   7. _____

4. _____

REVIEW EXERCISES FOR LESSONS 1 AND 2

1 Circle the letter of the best answer.

1. Which word is not derived from *ponere?*
   a. juxtapose   b. opponent   c. propinquity   d. interpose
   e. expound
2. Which word is not derived from *tithenai?*
   a. epithet   b. anathema   c. synthesis   d. epitome
   e. parenthesis
3. Which word is not derived from the root given?
   a. antithesis < *tithenai*
   b. abstruse < *trudere*
   c. internecine < *necare*
   d. unrequited < *quiescere*
   e. rapprochement < *ponere*
4. acquiesce : resist : :
   a. interpose : meddle
   b. juxtapose : join
   c. interpolate : omit
   d. obtrude : interfere
   e. requite : reciprocate
5. internecine : bloody : :
   a. peripatetic : sluggish
   b. eponymous : paradoxical
   c. quiescent : noisy
   d. altruistic : self-centered
   e. peripheral : insignificant

2 Matching: On the line at the left, write the letter of the phrase that provides the most appropriate example of the numbered word.

_____	**1.** paradox	A. a month-old newspaper
_____	**2.** epitaph	B. peace and war
_____	**3.** extrusion	C. a deer in the vegetable garden
_____	**4.** paradigm	D. Siamese twins
_____	**5.** antithesis	E. "To a [dead] Mouse"*
_____	**6.** requiem	F. "Gone but not forgotten"
_____	**7.** juxtaposition	G. 2 + 2 = 4
_____	**8.** interloper	H. Albert Einstein
_____	**9.** paragon	I. lava from a volcano
_____	**10.** ephemera	J. a Pyrrhic victory

3 Fill in each blank with the most appropriate word from Lessons 1 and 2. Use a word or any of its forms only once.

In his Pulitzer Prize–winning book *Guns, Germs, and Steel*, Jared Diamond attempts to explain why some cultures dominate others.

His explanation does not involve a) _____ (complex) social theory. Instead he applies a(n)

b) _____ (illustrative model) based on technology, epidemiology, and geography.

Diamond believes that when different cultures live in

c) _____ (proximity), they naturally assimilate from their neighbors whatever technologies they find useful, such as domestication of animals and plants, writing, shipbuilding, and navigation. The adoption of the horse by indigenous Americans

from European conquistadors d) _____ (provides a typical illustration of) this process.

e) _____ ly (With seeming contradiction), Native Americans also acquired contagious European diseases such as

_____

*Title of a poem by Robert Burns

smallpox and measles, which decimated their populations. Such
diseases contributed to the rapid f) _____
(consent without objection) of great empires like those of the Aztecs
and Incas to the will of Spanish invaders, who had tiny armies but superior technology and social organization.

Diamond illustrates the importance of geography by
g) _____ (placing side by side for
comparison) the east-west orientation of the Eurasian continent,
which permits easy migration within similar climate zones, to the
h) _____ (completely contrasting) north-south
orientation of the Americas and Africa, where deserts and jungles
make transfer of peoples and cultures difficult. He emphasizes
how throughout history, human populations have been
i) _____ (traveling about). For example, he
charts how culture and especially language show that most of the
peoples of the Pacific islands originated in China.

In Diamond's view, the dominance of the English language and
so-called Western culture in the world today is not the result of a
superior culture j) _____ (applying pressure,
interfering) itself on inferior cultures or genetically inferior peoples,
but the accidents of geography and botany.

4 Writing or Discussion Activities

1. Whom do you regard as a paragon, someone whose special style,
   talent, imagination, or spirit represents a high standard? Reflect on
   people you admire and choose one as the subject of a paragraph.
   Mention important details about the person, describe the person's
   attributes, and give reasons for your admiration.

2. Imagine yourself on a weekend outing—a camping or rafting trip—
   with one or more of the following companions. Think about the
   kind of specific behavior you might expect from each one. Choose
   one person and write a diary entry or a letter to a friend describing
   in colorful detail your remembered or imagined impression of such
   a person.
   a. an interloper
   b. an altruistic person
   c. an obtrusive person
   d. a peripatetic person
   e. a person who enjoys altercations

LESSONS 3 AND 4

Government

LESSON 3

Grex totus in agris unius scabie cadit.
A whole flock perishes in the fields from the mange of one sheep
(i.e., One diseased sheep spoils the flock).

Key Words		
aggregation	archive	gregarious
anarchy	demagogue	icon
archaic	demographer	iconoclastic
archetype	egregious	oligarchy
archipelago	endemic	pandemic

Familiar Words
archaeology
architecture
hierarchy
matriarch
monarch
patriarch

ARKHEIN <G. "to begin," "to be first"
ARKHOS <G. "ruler," "first in rank"

1. **archaic**   (är kā′ ĭk)
    adj. 1. Characteristic of a much earlier or primitive period.

    Anglo-Saxon, the **archaic** form of English, flourished in England for several hundred years before giving way to an influx of languages influenced by Latin.

    2. Antiquated; out-of-date.

    The scythe was made **archaic** by Cyrus McCormick's invention of the mechanical reaper in 1831.

    archaism, *n.*

2. **archetype**   (är´ kə tīp´)   [*tupos* <G. "mold," "model"]
   n. An original model or type from which similar forms are copied.

   Anthropologists have identified **archetypes** that appear in cultures throughout the world: the earth mother, the holy child, the wise old man, and the sky god or sun god.

   archetypal, *adj.*; **archetypic**, *adj.*; **archetypical**, *adj.*

3. **archipelago**   (är´ kə pĕl´ ə gō)   [*pelagos* <G. "sea"]
   n. 1. A group of many islands or the sea containing them.

   An **archipelago** of 1,150 islands in the South Pacific, the Marshall Islands gained independence from the United States in 1986.

   2. A group of separate entities contained within a defined area.

   Although Simon Bolívar dreamed of creating a single nation of the South American regions he helped to liberate from Spanish domination in the 1820s, today they remain an **archipelago** of individual states.

   archipelagic, *adj.*

4. **archive(s)**   (är´ kīvs´)
   n. (can be used in the singular or plural)
   The collected records of an organization, institution, or public person. (*Archives* can also refer to the place in which such records are stored.)

   Letters and papers in her **archives** reveal Emma Goldman's passionate belief in the right of citizens to criticize the constraints of unreasonable government.

   archival, *adj.*; **archivist**, *n.*

   NOTA BENE: In some cultures, archives prevail in other than written form. The Hmong peoples of southeast Asia, forbidden by their conquerors in the eighteenth century to use their written language, managed to record their history on colorful tapestries using embroidery and appliqué work. In western African communities a succession of elders called *griots* has served as a living archive of a people's oral history from its remembered beginnings.

5. **anarchy**   (ăn´ ər kē)   [*an* <G. "without"]
   n. 1. Absence of any form of government or political authority; lawlessness.

   In the opinion of Katherine Anne Porter, **anarchy** is harder for human beings to cope with than the greatest abuses and restrictions of an oppressive government.

2. Disorder and confusion.

Although the shipwrecked boys in *Lord of the Flies* at first attempt to govern themselves, their altercations lead to **anarchy** and self-destruction.

6. **oligarchy** (ŏl´ ə gär´ kē) [*oligos* <G. "few"]
n. Government by the few, especially a faction of persons or families.

In *The House of the Spirits* Isabel Allende describes a Chilean **oligarchy** composed of wealthy landowners who refuse to extend land rights to the peasants who work their haciendas.

oligarch, *n.*; **oligarchic**, *adj.*

NOTA BENE: The prefix *arch-* indicates "a chief of highest rank," as in *archangel* and *archbishop*; it can also mean "the first or ultimate of its kind," as in *archenemy* or *archfiend* (often Satan or the devil). The root *arch* in words like *patriarch* and *oligarch* means "leader" or "ruler." *Archy* indicates the form of "rule" or "government," as in *matriarchy* and *monarchy*.

Familiar Words
democracy
epidemic

Challenge Words
deme
demiurge
demos
demotic
epidemiology

DEMOS <G. "people"

7. **demagogue** (dĕm´ ə gôg´, dĕm´ ə gŏg´) [*apogos* <G. "leading"]
n. A leader or agitator who appeals to people's passions and prejudices rather than to their reason.

Willie Stark in *All the King's Men* resembles Huey P. Long, a **demagogue** who bullied and charmed his way to power as governor of Louisiana in the 1920s and 1930s.

demagogic, *adj.*; **demagogy**, *n.*

8. **demographer** (dĭ mŏg´ rə fər) [*graphein* <G. "to write"]
n. One who studies the characteristics of populations and analyzes data such as numbers, births, deaths, diseases, and other vital statistics.

Demographers have calculated from United States census figures that the center of the population in 1790 was east of Baltimore, Maryland; in 1890, near Columbia, Indiana; and in 1990, near Steelville, Missouri.

demography, *n.*; **demographic**, *adj.*

9. **endemic** (ĕn dĕm′ ĭk) [*en* <G. "in"]
adj. Commonly found in a particular region or among a particular people.

Before the draining of swamplands in the 1890s, malaria was **endemic** in southern Italy.

10. **pandemic** (păn dĕm′ ĭk) [*pan* <G. "all"]
adj. Spread throughout a wide geographic area; worldwide.

The disease known as AIDS, acquired immune deficiency syndrome, has become a **pandemic** threat since it was first identified in the 1980s.

> **NOTA BENE:** The Latin counterpart of the Greek root *demos*, "people," is *populus*, familiar in the derivatives *depopulate, pop* (as in pop art and music), *populace, popular,* and *popularity.* Also in general use is the Latin phrase *vox populi,* meaning "the voice of the people."

<table>
<tr><td>

Familiar Words
congregate
segregate

</td></tr>
</table>

GREX, GREGIS <L. "flock," "herd," "crowd"

11. **gregarious** (grĭ gâr′ ē əs)
adj. 1. Liking companionship; sociable.

Gertrude Stein's Paris salon, where **gregarious** American writers and artists gathered in the 1920s, became the center of the expatriate movement whose members Stein called "the lost generation."

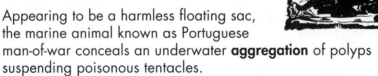

2. Tending to live or move in groups of one's own kind.

To Barry Lopez the thousands of **gregarious** snow geese fluidly rising and swirling above grain fields near Tule Lake in California resembled schools of fish above the ocean floor.

12. **aggregation** (ăg′ rə gā′ shən)
[*ag* = *ad* <L. "to," "toward"]
n. A large group or collection of people, animals, or things.

Appearing to be a harmless floating sac, the marine animal known as Portuguese man-of-war conceals an underwater **aggregation** of polyps suspending poisonous tentacles.

aggregate, *adj., n.,* and *v.*

13. **egregious** (ĭ grē′ jəs, ĭ grē′ jē əs) [*e* = *es* <L. "from," "out of"]
adj. Extraordinarily bad; flagrant.

Forty years after the discovery of Piltdown man was announced in 1912, this "missing link" in human evolution was proved to be an **egregious** hoax perpetrated by planting the bones of an orangutan with a modern human skull.

EIKON <G. "likeness," "image"

14. **icon**   (ī′ kŏn´)

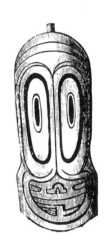

   n. 1. An image, representation, or symbol.

   Carved figures such as eagles, ravens, and whales that decorated interior and exterior poles of Haida dwellings in the Northwest were **icons** derived from myths and family crests.

   2. A representation or picture of a sacred personage or event, traditionally painted on wooden panels in the manner of Eastern Orthodox churches.

   The convention of Russian **icons** began in the tenth century when princes of Kiev brought back images from churches in Constantinople.

   3. A person greatly admired for a particular talent, quality, or service.

   Known as El Rey, the bandleader Tito Puente became an **icon** of Latino music combining jazz and Latin rhythms.

   NOTA BENE: Computer users are familiar with the term *icon* as a symbol for programs; in the days of hand presses, certain frequently-used pictorial blocks were also called icons.

15. **iconoclastic**   (ĭ kŏn´ ə klăs′ tĭk)   [*klasis* <G. "fracture"]
   adj. 1. Breaking or destroying images (referring especially to a movement to destroy images in Eastern Orthodox churches during the ninth and tenth centuries and a later Protestant movement).

   In sixteenth- and seventeenth-century Europe some **iconoclastic** Protestants smashed stained glass windows, beheaded religious statuary, and white-washed church murals in their effort to eradicate what they considered idolatry of sacred images.

   2. Attacking or overthrowing tradition or popular ideas, institutions, or conventions.

Challenge Words
iconography
iconolatry
iconology
iconoscope
iconostasis

As Charles Darwin sailed around South America on the *Beagle*, he developed his **iconoclastic** theory of evolution.

iconoclasm, *n.*, **iconoclast**, *n.*

EXERCISE 3A   Circle the letter of the best SYNONYM for the word in bold-faced type.

1. muscle strain **endemic** to runners   a. obtrusive   b. ephemeral   c. common   d. peripheral   e. helpful
2. a ruthless **demagogue**   a. mediator   b. eponym   c. interloper   d. fiery agitator   e. interregnum
3. **demographic** shifts in logging towns   a. environmental   b. recreational   c. political   d. working-class   e. population
4. a(n) **aggregation** of flamingos   a. throng   b. flight   c. altercation   d. scarcity   e. migration
5. a corrupt **oligarchy**   a. government by the rich   b. government by the many   c. government by the few   d. government by despot   e. monarchy
6. a political **iconoclast**   a. paragon   b. conservative   c. organizer   d. image breaker   e. radical
7. the **archetype** of the glider   a. epitome   b. antithesis   c. original   d. paradigm   e. copy
8. a(n) **anarchic** interregnum   a. unrequited   b. orderly   c. unlawful   d. disruptive   e. lawless
9. **egregious** actions   a. detestable   b. unrequited   c. admirable   d. solitary   e. internecine

Circle the letter of the best ANTONYM for the word in bold-faced type.

10. a(n) **pandemic** economic crisis   a. internecine   b. local   c. universal   d. devastating   e. quiescent
11. **gregarious** golfers   a. unfriendly   b. egregious   c. noisy   d. solitary   e. aggregate
12. **archaic** theories of nutrition   a. old-fashioned   b. altruistic   c. abstruse   d. reliable   e. avant-garde

EXERCISE 3B   Circle the letter of the sentence in which the word in bold-faced type is used incorrectly.

1. a. Scientific research has exonerated the people condemned at **egregious** witch trials in seventeenth-century Salem; the victims' "fault" lay in being solitary or eccentric in a highly conforming society.
   b. Gwendolyn Brooks's poem "Medgar Evers" pays tribute to the civil rights leader **egregiously** murdered in 1963.

    c. E pluribus unum, the motto on American coins, means "one out of many" or "**egregious**" ("from the herd").

    d. In *Gentlemen Prefer Blondes* Lorelei Lee supplies humor with **egregious** grammatical blunders such as "a girl like I."

2. a. Aleksandr Solzhenitsyn called the world's attention to the egregious detention of dissidents in forced labor camps, or *gulags*, scattered across the great **archipelago** of the former Soviet Union.

    b. As Peter Matthiessen traveled along Tierra del Fuego and smaller islands of the Chilean **archipelago**, he observed albatrosses, diving petrels, cormorants, terns, and skuas.

    c. The movement of tectonic plates that has reshaped continents has left **archipelagic** fragments clustering along coastlines.

    d. When choirs sing **archipelago**, without instrumental accompaniment, the singers must listen carefully to maintain proper pitch.

3. a. The reputation of the wise and altruistic Egyptian doctor Imhotep, an **icon** of the ancient world, attracted to his grave pilgrims looking for cures.

    b. When the Mongol conqueror Tamerlane unaccountably withdrew from attacking Moscow in 1389, Muscovites credited their preservation to the spiritual power of an **icon** borrowed from a neighboring town.

    c. **Iconic** designs of mythological beasts and fish decorated early Italian maps.

    d. In sculpting nonrepresentational **icons** from her imagination, Dame Barbara Hepworth used wood, stone, and bronze.

4. a. Classified as extinct in 1681 and eventually known only in illustrations, the odd, clumsy, earthbound dodo bird became mythical until scientists determined two hundred years later that the creature had been a real but **archaic** variety of pigeon.

    b. Athletes who have suffered severe injuries may experience **archaic** pain even after successful surgery.

    c. Computers today are far removed from the **archaic** models that required hand-fed punch cards, 500 miles of wire, and an entire building.

    d. Many English farmers continue the **archaic** practice of making a corn dolly, a female figure woven from the last sheaf of grain harvested in autumn and kept to be sown with the spring planting.

EXERCISE 3C   Fill in each blank with the most appropriate word from Lesson 3. Use a
word or any of its forms only once.

1. In *Animal Farm,* Napoleon becomes the _____
    of the barnyard, first uniting the animals in their hatred of the
    cruel farmer but then becoming equally cruel himself.
2. Depletion of forests to supply fuel or grazing land has become

    _____ , diminishing wildlife habitats and
    altering the quality of air worldwide.
3. The British House of Commons has been called the

    _____ of all parliamentary systems.

4. Data collected by _____ suggest that if the
    world population continues to increase at the present rate, it will
    outrun the planet's capacity to produce sufficient food.
5. After caribou calving season in northern Alaska,

    _____ of herds numbering as many as
    175,000 animals travel together before separating to head south
    for the winter.
6. Although the Communist government of the Soviet Union
    appeared to grant extensive power to party members,

    a(n) _____ of five party leaders who
    sat in the Politburo held ultimate authority.

7. Twyla Tharp has been called a(n) _____ for
    her playful choreography juxtaposing classical ballets and modern
    dance, described by one reviewer as "kinetic wisecracking."
8. Unlike American universities with defined campuses, Oxford and

    Cambridge Universities are academic _____ ,
    each having separate colleges located within the cities of Oxford
    and Cambridge.

9. Drought is _____ in equatorial Africa.
10. In the domestic culture of Zaire, families and friends are

    especially _____ at mealtimes, believing that
    eating is not intended to be a solitary activity.

11. Located in Washington, D.C., the National _____
    contains a vast collection of papers, books, and film pertaining to
    the history of the United States.
12. Okonkwo in *Things Fall Apart* struggles helplessly as he sees
    the dissolution of the old ways in his Ibo village and the

    _____ that results from colonial intrusion.

13. Opened to traffic in 1883 after numerous construction problems, the Brooklyn Bridge stands as an architectural

_____ of grace and utility.

EXERCISE 3D   Replace the word or phrase in italics with a key word (or any of its forms) from Lesson 3.

Often cited as perhaps the most (1) *flagrantly bad* miscarriage of American justice, the Sacco-Vanzetti case continues to draw historians to review documents in the (2) *collected records* of the court. Arrested in 1920 for two murders during a robbery, Nicola Sacco and Bartolomeo Vanzetti pleaded innocent. However, the defendants acknowledged at their trial that they were (3) *people who believe in abolishing government control* and were active in distributing pamphlets (4) *attacking traditional institutions* in their content. When the jury found the pair guilty, many supporters ascribing to Judge Webster Thayer the attitude of a (5) *prejudicial agitator* who was influenced by the "Red scare" (6) *commonly found* in the United States after the Russian Revolution in 1917.

Immediately before and after Sacco and Vanzetti were executed in 1927, (7) *huge throngs* of sympathizers protested throughout the world. Although for many partisans the case remains a(n) (8) *pattern from which similar forms are modeled* of justice denied, the most recent evidence from reexamination of trial records, ballistic tests, and belated confessions seems to support the original verdict: guilty.

1. _____   5. _____

2. _____   6. _____

3. _____   7. _____

4. _____   8. _____

LESSON 4

Rex regnat sed non gubernat.
A king reigns but does not govern.

Key Words		
annunciation	politic	regalia
conducive	polity	regency
exegesis	potentate	renunciation
hegemony	puissant	traduce
induce	redoubt	viceroy

DUCO, DUCERE, DUXI, DUCTUM
<L. "to lead"

1. **conducive**   (kən do͞o′ sĭv, kən dyo͞o′ sĭv)
   [*con = cum* <L. "with"]
   adj. Promoting; contributing (used with *to*); helpful.

   Katherine Dunham's training in anthropology was **conducive** to her acquiring a vast knowledge of dances and rituals of the Caribbean, which is reflected in her exotic choreography.

   conduce, *v.*; **conduciveness**, *n.*

2. **induce**   (ĭn do͞os′, ĭn dyo͞os′)   [*in* = <L. "in"]
   tr. v. 1. To persuade; to influence.

   The dull constraints of life as an unmarried Victorian woman **induced** Mary Kingsley to go to West Africa, where she spent two peripatetic years collecting scientific specimens.

   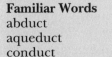

   2. To cause; to bring about.

   The obstetrician Ignaz Philipp Semmelweis proved in the 1840s that unsanitary conditions during delivery **induced** a deadly fever in new mothers, but many in the medical profession resisted any change to more sanitary practices for more than forty years.

   inducible, *adj.*; **inducement**, *n.*; **inducer**, *n.*

3. **traduce**   (trə do͞os′, trə dyo͞os′)   [*tra* = *trans* <L. "across"]
   tr. v. To slander; to speak falsely or maliciously of.

   Wrongly convicted of treason, Captain Alfred Dreyfus was imprisoned on Devil's Island from 1894 to 1899 until the disclosure of forged documents revealed that a group of anti-Semitic French officers had egregiously **traduced** him.

   traducer, *n.*

4. redoubt (rĭ dout′) [*re* = <L. "back," "again"]
n. 1. A small fort defending an important
point.

In the nineteenth century Russian fur traders
established Fort Ross, a **redoubt** on the
northern coast of California.

2. A place of refuge or defense.

During the Holocaust a large box in the Berlin apartment of Maria von
Maltzan became a **redoubt** for a Jewish friend whom she helped escape
from Nazi persecution.

HEGAISTHAI <G. "to lead"

5. hegemony (hĭ jĕm′ ə nē, hĕj′ ə mō′ nē)
n. Dominance, especially of one political body over another.

After **hegemony** over Tibet for centuries, China finally claimed it as
Chinese territory in 1951.

hegemonic, *adj.*

6. exegesis (ĕk′ sə jē′ sĭs; plural
exegeses) [*ex* <G. "from," "out of"]
n. A thorough explanation or
interpretation, especially of a sacred text.

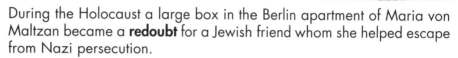

In her **exegesis** of the gnostic gospels,
ancient Christian texts not included in the
Bible, Elaine Pagels showed that both men
and women were leaders in many early
churches.

exegete, *n.*; **exegetic**, *adj.*; **exegetical**, *adj.*; **exegetics**, *n.*

NUNCIO, NUNCIARE, NUNCIAVI, NUNCIATUM
<L. "to announce"

7. annunciation (ə nŭn′ sē ā′ shən) [*an* = *ad* "to," "toward"]
n. 1. An announcement; a proclamation.

Eduardo Galeano ironically observes that in 1890 the Sioux peoples
at Wounded Knee celebrated "the **annunciation** of paradise, the end of
hunger and exile" just before soldiers killed many of the celebrants.

2. (often capitalized) In Christian thought, the announcement by the angel Gabriel to Mary that she would give birth to the son of God.

The **Annunciation** was the subject of many early Renaissance paintings and was often portrayed by an angel kneeling before Mary with a stalk of white lilies in his hand as a dove flew overhead.

annunciate, *v.*; **annunciator**, *n.*

8. **renunciation**   (rĭ nŭn´ sē ā´ shən)   [*re* <L. "back," "again"] *n.* An action or statement in which something is given up, rejected, abandoned, or sacrificed.

Charlotte Mary May's recognition of a debilitating hereditary illness in her family led to her **renunciation** of marriage and motherhood.

renunciative, *adj.*, **renunciatory**, *adj.*

POLIS <G. "city"
POLITIKOS <G. "citizen"

City

9. **polity**   (pŏl´ ĭ tē) *n.* An organized society, such as a nation, state, church, or other organization, having a specific form of government.

European interlopers in Africa and South America during the nineteenth century were egregiously insensitive to the existence of native **polities**.

10. **politic**   (pŏl´ ə tĭk) *adj.* 1. Wise; prudent; sagacious.

Deft and **politic**, Eleanor Roosevelt brought to fruition the Universal Declaration of Human Rights, adopted by the United Nations in 1948.

2. Expedient; taking advantage of the moment; shrewd.

When King Lear tests the love of his three daughters before divesting himself of his kingdom, two are **politic** and insincere and win his favor; the youngest, declaring that she will divide her love between her father and her husband, is disowned.

Antonym: **impolitic**

NOTA BENE: *Politic* meaning "policy-making" appears in the phrase "body politic" or "political body": "As there are mountebanks for the natural body, so are there mountebanks for the politic body."—Francis Bacon

POSSUM, POSSE, POTUI <L. "to be able," "to have power"

Familiar Words
impossible
impotent
omnipotent
possible
potent
potential

Challenge Words
plenipotentiary
prepotent

11. **potentate**   (pōt′ n tāt′)
    n. Monarch; a ruler possessing great power.

    When India became part of the British Empire in 1858, the regional **potentates**, or maharajas, lost their power.

12. **puissant**   (pwĭs′ ənt, pyōō′ ə sənt,
    pyōō ĭs′ ənt)
    adj. Mighty; powerful; forceful.

    "Methinks I see in my mind a noble and **puissant** nation rousing herself like a strong man after sleep, and shaking her invincible locks."—John Milton (speaking of England, 1644)

    puissance, *n.*

REX, REGIS <L. "king"

Familiar Words
interregnum
regal
regularity
regulation
reign
Rex
royal

Challenge Words
interrex
Regius Professor
regulus
vicereine

13. **regalia**   (rĭ găl′ yə, rī gā′ lē ə)   (plural in form but often used as a singular noun)
    n. 1. Emblems and symbols of royalty, rank, office, or institution.

    "A trade school in a poor community seldom has archaic **regalia** or ritual, but a school aimed at education of the leisure class . . . will generally have . . . features such as medieval gowns and elaborate Latin degree ceremonies."—Thorstein Veblen

    2. Finery; elaborate attire.

    High school prom nights often require formal **regalia**: tuxedos with satin lapels and matching cummerbunds for young men, and elegant gowns, corsages, and long gloves for young women.

14. **regency**   (rē′ jən sē)
    n. The office or period of office of a regent; one who administers for a monarch, especially (sometimes capitalized) in England (1811–1820) and in France (1715–1723).

    When George III was declared insane, the Prince of Wales assumed the **regency**, becoming George IV at his father's death in 1820.

    adj. and *n.* (often capitalized) A style of dress, furniture, and architecture characteristic of the regency period in England.

    Interior decoration in the English **Regency** style incorporated Greek and Roman features, Egyptian motifs, and Chinese lacquer designs.

    regent, *n.*

15. **viceroy**   (vīs′ roi′)   [*vice = uice* <L. "in place of"]
    n. A governor or ruler exercising authority on behalf of a sovereign in a province or colony.

    Because of the great distance between Spain and the New World, a series of sixty-two **viceroys** exerted much independent power over Spain's territory in Mexico between 1535 and 1824.

EXERCISE 4A

Circle the letter of the best SYNONYM for the word(s) in bold-faced type.

1. graduation **regalia**   a. diplomas   b. speeches   c. symbolic attire   d. reunions   e. celebrations
2. attacking a **redoubt**   a. weak point   b. military guard   c. gun installation   d. small fort   e. change of mind
3. a brilliant **exegesis**   a. criticism   b. interpretation   c. summary d. annunciation   e. defense
4. a surprising **annunciation**   a. decree   b. invitation   c. declaration d. sacrifice   e. anathema
5. a gregarious **viceroy**   a. vice president   b. regent   c. political advisor   d. interim potentate   e. colonial governor
6. a(n) **puissant** demagogue   a. arrogant   b. weak   c. powerful d. obtrusive   e. politic
7. a life **conducive to** thrift   a. discouraging   b. promoting c. accelerating   d. mocking   e. reproaching
8. **traduced** by a trusted friend   a. kidnapped   b. tricked   c. praised d. defamed   e. employed
9. to anticipate **renunciation**   a. denial   b. departure   c. reproach d. acceptance   e. rejection
10. the **polity** of the European Community   a. oligarchy b. hegemony   c. organization   d. anarchy   e. exegesis

Circle the letter of the best ANTONYM for the word in bold-faced type.

11. a(n) **hegemonic** relationship   a. subordinate   b. equal
    c. impolitic   d. exegetic   e. quiescent
12. to **induce** cooperation   a. demand   b. encourage   c. express
    d. interpose   e. stifle
13. an acquiescent **potentate**   a. explorer   b. monarch   c. peon
    d. politician   e. prizefighter
14. a(n) **politic** reply   a. clever   b. naive   c. political   d. peripheral
    e. obtrusive

EXERCISE 4B   Circle the letter of the sentence in which the word in bold-faced type is used incorrectly.

1. a. Early icons of the **Annunciation** traditionally depict the angel
   Gabriel on the left and the Virgin Mary on the right showing
   surprise or acceptance at the news of her imminent motherhood.
   b. Stage actresses like Helen Hayes and Lynn Fontanne learned
   early in their careers the dramatic effect of clarity and crispness
   in **annunciation**.
   c. The official **annunciation** of the end of World War I occurred at
   the eleventh hour of the eleventh day of the eleventh month of
   1918.
   d. The **annunciation** of the defeat of the Persians in 400 B.C. was
   made by Pheidippides, who ran twenty-six miles from the plain
   of Marathon to Athens.
2. a. Admiring her poetry and falling in love with the poet, Robert
   Browning **induced** Elizabeth Barrett to elope with him.
   b. Many teachers and parents have tried to **induce** left-handed
   children to become right-handed, not realizing the harm caused
   by changing a biologically determined impulse.
   c. More than one method can **induce** relaxation: soft music,
   meditation, exercise, or a good book.
   d. In the opera *The Elixir of Love*, the mountebank Dulcamara
   induces a potion guaranteed to make purchasers irresistible to
   the opposite sex.
3. a. Following the assassination in 1610 of her husband, King Henry
   IV of France, Marie de' Medici assumed the **regency** of her son
   Louis XIII until he forced her into retirement in 1617.
   b. Fashionable women of the English **Regency** period wore dresses
   that imitated the high-waisted "empire" style introduced by the
   French empress Josephine.
   c. In 1950 the Swedish activist Alva Myrdal became the **regency** of
   the Social Science division of the United Nations Educational,
   Scientific, and Cultural Organization (UNESCO).

   d. Because King Louis XIV died when his great-grandson and heir
      was only five years old, a **regent** performed state services until
      young Louis XV reached the age of thirteen.

4. a. Although stories by Horatio Alger now seem excessively
      moralistic, the author's advice to be **politic** whenever there is a
      chance to advance oneself sounds contemporary.
   b. Clara Shortridge Foltz, the first woman admitted to practice law
      in California, played an active role in **politic** and government
      issues throughout her life.
   c. Niccolò Machiavelli's **politic** advice to an Italian prince was to let
      goals justify the means of obtaining them.
   d. Although Nora Helmer believes she has been **politic** in hiding
      her financial arrangements from her husband, she has naively
      disregarded the legal consequences of her forgery.

EXERCISE 4C   Fill in each blank with the most appropriate word from Lesson 4. Use a
                    word or any of its forms only once.

1. Bernadette Devlin's experience as an Irish politician taught her a

   meaning of _____: "To gain that which is
   worth having, it may be necessary to lose everything else."

2. Discovering when he was very ill that laughter was

   _____ to recovery, Norman Cousins took
   regular doses of humor from radio comedians and funny films.

3. Although Helen Gahagan Douglas lost her bid for a U.S. Senate

   seat in 1950 because her opponent _____
   her as a Communist sympathizer, she says she emerged from
   defeat without resentment.

4. Lord Louis Mountbatten of Burma was appointed by King George

   VI to serve as _____ of India during its last
   year of British colonial rule.

5. In *The Devil's Dictionary* the satirist Ambrose Bierce defines

   _____ as "the distinguishing insignia, jewels,
   and costumes of such ancient and honorable orders as . . . The
   Sublime Legion of Flamboyant Conspicuants . . . and the Mysterious
   Order of the Indecipherable Scroll."

6. Although well known for her mystery stories, Dorothy Sayers was

   also noted for her _____ of Dante's *The
   Divine Comedy.*

7. Sherwood Forest became a(n) _____ for Robin Hood and his followers, protecting them from forays by the Sheriff of Nottingham.

8. As a(n) _____ known as an "enlightened despot" because she encouraged Western ideas, Czarina Catherine the Great of Russia nonetheless followed the ruthless pattern of her predecessors.

9. A hero of the Zulu peoples, Chaka demonstrated his

_____ early, reorganizing the army and drawing into the Zulu many clans that he had subjugated.

10. Occupied by Soviet forces in 1940, Latvia, Lithuania, and Estonia

fell under the _____ of the Soviet Union, regaining their independence only after the collapse of its Communist government.

11. Unlike other Renaissance city states ruled by princes, Venice was

a _____ controlled by an oligarchy of wealthy merchants.

12. Often neoclassical, the _____ style can include such exotic forms as the rooflines of Moorish onion-domes and the Chinese furnishings of the Royal Pavilion at Brighton, England.

EXERCISE 4D   Replace the word or phrase in italics with a key word (or any of its forms) from Lesson 4.

Seventeenth-century settlers in North America made a(n) (1) *prudent* gesture of eponymously honoring their monarchs by naming the colony of Virginia after the (2) *very powerful* Virgin Queen Elizabeth I and Jamestown, the first permanent settlement, after King James I.

By the 1760s and 1770s, however, the Sugar Act, Stamp Act, tea tax, and other monetary pressures (3) *influenced* the colonists to rebel against the (4) *political dominance* of the British crown. The Declaration of Independence in 1776 was the official (5) *announcement* of American intent to be free from foreign (6) *monarchs*. When the name of General George Washington circulated as that of a likely king, he refused that office and its (7) *symbols of status*, the crown and scepter, asserting his faith in electoral democracy. In 1787 representatives of the federation of states met in Philadelphia to shape the (8) *national government* of their new republic; four months later they had composed the Constitution of the United States. In 1789, a Bill of Rights was added.

1. _____   5. _____
2. _____   6. _____
3. _____   7. _____
4. _____   8. _____

REVIEW EXERCISES FOR LESSONS 3 AND 4

1 Circle the letter of the best answer.

1. Which of the following words does not refer to an authorized
   government official?
   a. oligarch   b. potentate   c. viceroy   d. anarchist   e. regent
2. Which of the following words is not derived from *ducere?*
   a. deduction   b. conducive   c. endemic   d. duchess   e. redoubt
3. Which of the following words is not derived from *demos?*
   a. demagogue   b. condemnation   c. democrat   d. pandemic
   e. demography
4. archaic : modern : :
   a. pandemic : worldwide
   b. anarchic : independent
   c. iconoclastic : traditional
   d. gregarious : congenial
   e. politic : canny
5. archipelago : islands : :
   a. regalia : emblems
   b. archetype : models
   c. icon : paintings
   d. archive : documents
   e. polity : hegemonies
6. anarchist : lawless : :
   a. demagogue : egregious
   b. iconoclast : gregarious
   c. viceroy : conducive
   d. potentate : powerful
   e. oligarch : endemic
7. aggregate : to flock together : :
   a. conduce : to promote
   b. annunciate : to keep silent
   c. traduce : to hold in esteem
   d. renounce : to restate
   e. induce : to create obstacles

2 Matching: On the line at the left, write the letter of the phrase that best illustrates the numbered phrase.

_____ **1.** the puissance of a demagogue

_____ **2.** an archive of icons

_____ **3.** a redoubt of anarchists

_____ **4.** the hegemony of a potentate

_____ **5.** an aggregation in academic regalia

_____ **6.** the renunciation of a polity

A. the domination of a monarch

B. the power of a ruthless leader

C. the rejection of an organized society

D. a crowd of people in caps and gowns

E. a collection of sacred paintings

F. headquarters of friends of Sacco and Vanzetti

3 Fill in each blank with the most appropriate word from Lessons 3 and 4. Use a word or any of its forms only once.

The a) _____ (ancient) Greek city-states have long been cited as the b) _____ (original model) for modern democratic governments. While nearby countries like Persia and Egypt were ruled by all-powerful c) _____s (monarchs), conditions on the Greek mainland and d) _____es (groups of islands) were e) _____ (promoting) to the development of a(n) f) _____ (social organization) where all free men had a voice in their government.

However, scholars often fail to note that this cherished g) _____ (image, representation) of democratic government was in fact a(n) h) _____ (government of the few) that i) _____ (flagrantly) excluded at least two-thirds of the population, including all women and slaves. Although early democracies in Europe and North America were similar j) _____ies (domination by one group) of privileged males, continual reforms have extended the idea of democracy to mean participation in government by all adult citizens.

4   Writing or Discussion Activities

1. Regalia, with its insignia, colors, or fancy design, identifies people as belonging to a particular group. If you or someone you know wears such clothing as a member of a team, organization, or group, write a paragraph describing this regalia so that a stranger could visualize its detail, design, color, and texture, know your feelings about it, and sense the reactions of others to it.

2. Exercise 4D above refers to the Bill of Rights drawn up in 1789 by the first Congress to define the rights and responsibilities of citizens and their government. Compose a statement of the rights and responsibilities of students in your classroom: "The right of students shall be . . ." or "The rights of students shall include. . . ."

LESSONS 5 AND 6

Up and Down

LESSON 5

Leve fit, quod bene fertur, onus.
A burden that is cheerfully borne is made light.—OVID

Key Words

bas-relief	leaven	penchant
debase	legerdemain	ponderous
declivity	leverage	preponderant
echelon	levitate	proclivity
imponderable	levity	transcendent

Familiar Words
base
basement
basis
bass
basset hound
bassoon

Challenge Words
abase
basso
basso-profundo
basso-relievo

BASIS <G. "pedestal," "foot," "base"
BASSUS <L. "low"

1. **bas-relief**   (bä′ rĭ lēf′)   [*rilevo* <Italian "relief"]
   n. Sculpture whose ornament or figures are
   somewhat raised above the background
   (also known as "low relief").

   Trajan's column, which stands in Rome,
   is encircled with **bas-reliefs** depicting the
   emperor's military victories.

   bas-relief, *adj.*

2. **debase** (dĭ bās′)   [*de* <L. "away from"]
   tr. v. To lower in quality, value, or dignity; to degrade.

   According to Flora Tristán, the llama is the only animal that human beings have not been able to **debase** because it refuses to be mistreated or to take orders.

Challenge Word
acclivity

CLIVUS <L. "slope"

3. **declivity** (dĭ klĭv′ ə tē)
   [*de* <L. "away from"]
   n. A downward slope; the slope of a hill.

   Undersea photographs of the floor of the
   Atlantic Ocean reveal **declivities** that
   resemble topographical configurations on land.

   declivitous, *adj.*

4. **proclivity** (prō klĭv′ ə tē)   [*pro* <L. "forth"]
   n. A natural inclination or tendency.

   "By necessity, by **proclivity**, and by delight, we all quote."
   —Ralph Waldo Emerson

   proclivitous, *adj.*

Familiar Words
alleviate
elevate
lever
light
relieve

Challenge Words
alto-relievo
basso-relievo
Levant
levee
mezzo-relievo

LEVIS <L. "light (in weight)"

5. **leaven** (lĕv′ ən)
   n. 1. A substance like yeast or a small amount of fermented dough that causes dough to expand or rise.

   In *My Ántonia* Mrs. Shimerda shocks her American neighbors by her old-country method of using fermented dough as a **leaven** for new loaves of bread.

   2. A lightening or enlivening influence.

   The film critic Penelope Gilliatt admires Judy Holliday and Marilyn Monroe for the **leaven** they impart as "beautiful clowns," smarter than everyone else and knowing that they will eventually be found out.

   tr. v. To provide a lightening influence.

   Letters from home **leaven** the spirits of battle-weary troops.

6. **legerdemain** (lĕj′ ər də mān′)   [*leger de main*
   <French "quick of hand" <L. *levis de manu*]
   n. 1. Sleight of hand; magic tricks.

   Thomas Betson, a fifteenth-century monk
   skilled in **legerdemain**, could make a hollow
   egg appear to float by suspending it below
   his hand with a fine hair.

2. Any trickery or deception.

Emmeline Piggott, a Confederate spy who epitomized the elegant Southern belle, easily slipped military documents past Union sentries through the **legerdemain** of concealing the messages under her voluminous hoopskirt.

7. **leverage** (lĕv′ ər ĭj, lē′ vər ĭj)
n. 1. The action of a lever that raises or lifts.

The **leverage** of an automobile jack enables a person to raise a heavy vehicle.

2. Power to influence; a position of strength.

During her tenure as the British prime minister, Margaret Thatcher applied **leverage** to her conservative cabinet by appointing ministers who agreed with her policies.

8. **levitate** (lĕv′ ə tāt′)
tr. and *intr. v.* To rise or float, or cause to rise, seemingly despite gravity.

Tests in Germany and Japan have proved that instead of moving on wheels, high-speed trains can **levitate** on a cushion of magnetic force.

levitation, *n.*

9. **levity** (lĕv′ ə tē)
n. Lightness in speech or behavior, especially unbecoming jocularity; frivolity.

Tess Durbeyfield disdains the **levity** of the young village women whose chief pleasure is dancing on Saturday night and sleeping off on Sunday the effects of their indulgence in "curious compounds."

NOTA BENE: Dictionaries give *levity* a second definition, "lightness in weight"; however, scientific usage requires *buoyancy* when applied to objects in water, or *density* when they are weighed.

The Latin antonym of *levis*, "light," is *gravis*, "heavy," from which come many familiar words, among them *aggravate, gravitate, grave*, and *grief*. The opposite of *levity* is *gravity*, "seriousness" or "weightiness." In its literal sense *gravity* is what causes objects to have weight.

PENDO, PENDERE, PEPENDI, PENSUM
<L. "to cause to hang down," "to weigh"
PONDERO, PONDERARE, PONDERAVI,
PONDERATUM <L. "to weigh"

10. **penchant** (pĕn' chənt)
    n. A strong inclination or liking.

    Niara Sudarkasa's **penchant** as a college student for facts about Africa led her to focus her career on African anthropology.

    NOTA BENE: Although *penchant* and *proclivity* may seem similar in meaning, they function differently. A penchant is a preference for something; dogs may have a *penchant*, or fondness, for bones and a *proclivity*, or inclination, to bark at the mail carrier. A *proclivity* is an inner impulse or direction, a characteristic action: a *proclivity* for altruism, spending money, or fatalism, for example.

11. **ponderous** (pŏn' dər əs)
    adj. 1. Extremely heavy; massive.

    Although they lacked wheeled vehicles, the Incas moved **ponderous** stones across high Andean passes to build cities like Machu Picchu.

    2. Unwieldly or awkward.

    The **ponderous** galleons of the Spanish Armada were no match for the light, fast British ships, able to strike and then dart out of firing range.

    3. Dull or tedious.

    The *Pilgrim's Progress* may seem **ponderous** to some readers because of its heavily moral tone, but it remains the epitome of literary allegory.

12. **imponderable** (ĭm pŏn' dər ə bəl)   [*im = in* <L. "not"]
    adj. Unable to be assessed or measured precisely.

    Although scientists can plan most aspects of a space flight accurately, the weather for launch and reentry remains an **imponderable** factor.

    Antonym: **ponderable**

13. **preponderant** (prĭ pŏn' dər ənt)   [*pre* <L. "before"]
    adj. Superior in number, force, power, or importance.

    Introduced from South America only in the sixteenth century, the potato has become the **preponderant** food source for much of Europe, the Americas, and Africa.

    preponderance, *n.*; **preponderate**, *v.*

| **Familiar Words** |
| condescend |
| descend |
| descendant |
| escalate |
| escalator |
| scale (*n.* and *v.*) |

| **Challenge Words** |
| escalade |
| scandent |
| scansion |
| Transcendentalism |

SCALA <L. "steps," "stairs," "ladder," "scale"
SCANDO, SCANDERE, SCANDI, SCANSUM <L. "to climb"

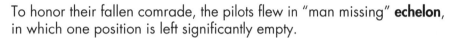

14. **echelon** (ĕsh′ ə lŏn′) [*echelon* <French "rung of a ladder"]
n. 1. A step-like formation of troops, ships, or aircraft.

To honor their fallen comrade, the pilots flew in "man missing" **echelon**, in which one position is left significantly empty.

2. A level of command or authority.

Promoted in 1970 to the rank of brigadier general in the Women's Army Corps, Elizabeth P. Hoisington and Anna Mae Hays became the first women to reach that **echelon** in the United States Armed Forces.

15. **transcendent** (trăn sĕn′ dənt) [*trans* <L. "across"]
adj. Going beyond the limits of ordinary experience.

To Emily Dickinson everyday occurrences like seeing a snake, a clover, or a "slant of light" became **transcendent**, leading her to reflect on natural law and mortality.

transcendence, *n.*; **transcendental**, *adj.*

NOTA BENE: The word *transcendental* has a meaning similar to that of *transcendent*: "rising above common thought or ideas." *Transcendental* also has a more philosophical meaning: "asserting a supernatural or mystical element in experience." In the 1860s a group of New Englanders known as Transcendentalists believed in the presence of God in nature and placed great faith in individualism and self-reliance, especially as expressed by Ralph Waldo Emerson, Margaret Fuller, and Henry David Thoreau.

EXERCISE 5A

Circle the letter of the best SYNONYM for the word(s) in bold-faced type.

1. an occasion for **levity**   a. leverage   b. insults   c. gravity
   d. powerful action   e. frivolity
2. a border of **bas-relief** figures   a. slightly raised   b roughened
   c. engraved   d. three-dimensional   e. silhouetted

3. a **ponderous** first novel　a. complex　b. thoughtful　c. boring
d. thought-provoking　e. straightforward
4. a(n) **imponderable** outcome　a. believable　b. difficult
c. calculable　d. indeterminable　e. unthinkable
5. to **debase** an opponent　a. insult　b. humiliate　c. exalt
d. surpass　e. traduce
6. a precarious **declivity**　a. debasement　b. quiescence　c. slope
d. cliff　e. loss of power
7. **levitation** of a table　a. lightening　b. lowering　c. motion
d. floating　e. reconstruction
8. the **leverage** of public opinion　a. imponderability
b. powerlessness　c. influence　d. acquiescence
e. transcendence
9. to add **leaven** to the discussion　a. suspense　b. meat
c. ponderousness　d. relevance　e. levity
10. the potentate's **legerdemain**　a. accuracy　b. honesty
c. deception　d. sense of humor　e. grouchiness

Circle the best ANTONYM for the word in bold-faced type.

11. a **proclivity** for sports　a. disinclination　b. fondness
c. tendency　d. penchant　e. polity
12. the **preponderance** of reporters　a. exclusion　b. bias
c. debasement　d. obtrusiveness　e. shortage
13. a(n) **transcendent** moment　a. antithetical　b. egregious
c. ordinary　d. iconoclastic　e. quiescent
14. a **penchant** for the archaic　a. proclivity　b. preference
c. longing　d. distaste　e. priority

EXERCISE 5B

Circle the letter of the sentence in which the word in bold-faced type is used incorrectly.

1. a. The bison clambered **ponderously** over the hill.
   b. Rodin's sculpture *The Thinker*, with elbow on his knee and hand under his chin, expresses a **ponderous** attitude.
   c. The demagogues' lengthy sentences and abstract language grew more **ponderous** the longer they talked.
   d. Although Howard Hughes had high expectations for his eight-engine wooden flying boat designed to carry 750 passengers, the **ponderous** *Spruce Goose* flew just one mile on its first and only voyage.
2. a. The peripatetic Jenkinses, Peter and Barbara, traveled the **transcendent** route across America, from Louisiana to Washington state.

Damian Hernandez

→ transparent

(translucent) → "lucere" - to shine
↳ clear

lghts → (illuminate) → "lumen" - to shine
↳ ill ↳ bright

& (monster) → "montrare" → point out
↳ different

offended → (appall) → "pallere" → to become pale
↳ disgusted
↳ shocked

(enlighten) → synonym =
↳ clear

    b. Giuseppe Verdi enjoyed what must have been a **transcendent** moment when he took thirty-two curtain calls after a performance of *Aida*.

    c. When Helen Keller, deaf and mute from age two, finally learned to speak, she **transcended** her incapacities by attending college and writing about her life.

    d. As Gabriel García Márquez guides readers to a Caribbean village in *One Hundred Years of Solitude*, he provides reality, but he also **transcends** it by collapsing the limitations of time and space through the device of "magic realism."

3. a. After losing the case at the state court of appeals, the lawyers appealed to the next legal **echelon**, the Supreme Court.

    b. For mutual protection, convoys of transport ships crossed the Atlantic during World War II in close **echelon**, flanked by destroyers and submarines.

    c. The honor guard stood at **echelon** during the ceremony.

    d. Japanese management encourages workers from every **echelon** in the company to offer new ideas for production and efficiency.

4. a. A cook adds baking powder, a **leavening** agent, to cornmeal to make cornbread but omits **leavening** to prepare tortillas.

    b. The candidate **leavened** the campaign speech by performing some extempore legerdemain with a deck of cards.

    c. The **leavening** properties of carbonated beverages are at their peak just as a bottle or can is opened.

    d. In memory of the Hebrews who had to leave Egypt in haste before their bread had risen, Jewish tradition proscribes the use of **leaven** in bread during the Passover holiday.

5. a. In the play *Blithe Spirit* Madame Arcati, an expert in seances and **legerdemain**, induces a deceased wife to appear to her former husband but to be annoyingly invisible to his second wife.

    b. Amateur practitioners of **legerdemain** usually begin by displacing coins and making handkerchiefs disappear before moving on to suspending a glass in midair.

    c. Moviegovers today take for granted the **legerdemain** of special effects, such as the juxtaposition of human actors with cartoon characters.

    d. For **legerdemain** during a hot summer, travel agencies suggest a cruise to Alaska.

EXERCISE 5C   Fill in each blank with the most appropriate word from Lesson 5. Use a word or any of its forms only once.

    1. Once a famous child movie star, Shirley Temple Black rose to the

        highest diplomatic _____ as ambassador to Ghana and later to the Czech Republic.

2. According to the Koran, King Solomon owned a carpet that

   _____ at his command and, with the help of wind, sped wherever he directed it.

3. During World War II women were _____ in the work force, symbolized by Rosie the Riveter.

4. The Elgin Marbles, sculpted in _____ and originally forming a border around the Parthenon of Athens, are now on display in the British Museum in London.

5. Although we can calculate the geologic forces that created the earth's past and existing features, the development of future

   mountain ranges, volcanoes, and oceans is _____.

6. Following World War I the _____ of most European currencies became so extreme that a loaf of bread could cost a day's wages.

7. Fundamental to business strategy is advantageous

   _____ of maximum financial return and the constants of energy, time, and investments.

8. Margaret Walker Alexander's _____ for poetry developed in her childhood when her father read to her and told her that poetry must have pictures, music, and meaning.

9. As the last North American glacier retreated to the north,

   it left _____ and basins that became tens of thousands of lakes, including the five Great Lakes.

10. By their _____ for treachery and cruelty, the notorious Cesare Borgia and his sister Lucrezia demonstrated their propinquity in both character and kinship.

11. There was instant _____ at the children's concert when a string snapped on the soloist's violin.

EXERCISE 5D   Replace the word or phrase in italics with a key word (or any of its forms) from Lesson 5.

When the circus comes to town, parents and children indulge their (1) *liking* for spectacles under the big top to (2) *lighten* the summer doldrums. Red-nosed clowns induce (3) *frivolity* when they (4) *make fools of* themselves by stumbling over their outsize shoes, sprawling in the dust, and then showing off their (5) *magic tricks* by producing pigeons from their tall hats. In another ring (6) *massive* elephants march and prance at their trainer's command. The crowd gasps as gymnasts form a human pyramid, each (7) *step in the formation* creating (8) *incalculable* weight.

Finally, near the roof, trapeze artists swoop from swing to swing, hand to hand, (9) *going beyond ordinary experience* in their apparent (10) *defiance of gravity.*

1. _____   6. _____

2. _____   7. _____

3. _____   8. _____

4. _____   9. _____

5. _____   10. _____

LESSON 6

Nil sub sole novum.
[There is] nothing new under the sun.—Ecclesiastes

Key Words		
aver	incumbent	subterfuge
cataclysm	recumbent	succumb
catapult	subjective	verisimilitude
hypochondria	sublimate	verity
hypothesis	suborn	

Familiar Words
cube
cubicle
cubism
incubate

Challenge Words
accumbent
cubit
decumbent

CUBO, CUBARE, CUBUI, CUBITUM
<L. "to lie down"
INCUMBO, INCUMBERE, INCUBUI, INCUBITUM <L. "to recline"

1. **incumbent** (ĭn kŭm′ bənt)   [*in* <L. "in"]
   n. A person who holds an office or position.

   An **incumbent** in the U.S. Congress for thirty-two years, Margaret Chase Smith served longer than any other woman.

   adj. 1. Already holding an office or position.

   Incumbent school board members may stand a better chance in an election than their inexperienced challengers.

   2. Required as a duty or obligation (often used with *on*).

   It is **incumbent** on all parents of school-age children to have them vaccinated for measles, mumps, and polio.

   incumbency, *n.*

NOTA BENE: *Incumbent* is sometimes used in its literal sense, "leaning" or "lying on" as in, Crumbling rock and *incumbent* slabs of stone and concrete made rescue efforts after the earthquake both difficult and hazardous.

2. **recumbent**   (rĭ kŭm′ bənt)   [*re* <L. "back," "again"]
adj. Reclining; lying down.

Although they quarreled fiercely in life, the **recumbent** effigies of Eleanor of Aquitaine and King Henry II of England now rest pacifically side by side on their tombs.

recumbence, *n.*; **recumbency**, *n.*

3. **succumb**   (sə kŭm′)   [*suc* = *sub* <L. "under"]
intr. v. 1. To yield; to give in or give up, especially to a powerful force or desire (often used with *to*).

The major sorrow of young Werther's life is his unrequited passion for Charlotte, who gently but firmly refuses to **succumb** to his many protestations of love.

2. To die.

Until 1882 when Robert Koch, a German physician, identified the tiny bacillus causing tuberculosis, its victims expected to **succumb** quickly.

HUPO <G. "under," "beneath"

4. **hypochondria**   (hī′ pə kŏn′ drē ə)
[*khondros* <G. "cartilege"]
n. A psychological disorder characterized by the illusory conviction that one is ill or in pain, or likely to become so.

Jane Austen's novel *Emma* depicts **hyponchondria** humorously, as Mr. Woodhouse encourages guests to join him in eating wholesome gruel and fears the effect of bad weather upon his health.

hypochondriac, *n.*; **hypochondriacal**, *adj.*

NOTA BENE: The word *hypochondria* contains a compressed form of archaic medical theory. According to ancient Greek and medieval diagnosis, feelings of melancholy, caused by the humor "melancholy," and delusions of illness had their source in the abdomen (for which

<table>
<tr><td>

Challenge Words
hypogastric
hypoglossia
hypoglycemia
hypoplasia
hypostasis
hypothecate
hypothyroid

</td><td>

the Greek word is *hupokhondrium*), located "under the cartilage" of the breastbone. Consequently *hypochondria,* in English, still has its source "under the cartilage."

5. hypothesis (hĭ pŏth′ ə sĭs)   [*tithenai* <G. "to put"]
n. 1. A theory or explanation that leads to further investigation for proof or disproof.

Although the **hypothesis** that all of the Indo-European family of languages derive from one original language is widely accepted, it will probably never be proven because this extinct language existed before the invention of writing.

2. An assumption on which a conclusion or decision is based.

"The great tragedy of Science—the slaying of a beautiful **hypothesis** by an ugly fact."—T.H. Huxley

hypothesize, *v.;* **hypothetical,** *adj.*

</td></tr>
</table>

KATA <G. "down"

<table>
<tr><td>

Familiar Words
catacomb
catalog
catalyst
cataract
catastrophe

</td><td>

6. cataclysm (kăt′ ə klĭz′ əm)   [*kluzein* <G. "to wash"]
n. A disaster or catastrophe on such a large scale that biological, environmental, or cultural elements are permanently altered or irreparably lost to the earth.

A **cataclysm** that occurred sixty-five million years ago changed atmospheric conditions so drastically that no dinosaurs were able to survive.

cataclysmal, *adj.;* **cataclysmic,** *adj.*

</td></tr>
<tr><td>

Challenge Words
catacoustics
catafalque
catalepsy
catamenia
catarrh

</td><td>

NOTA BENE: Some dictionaries give overlapping definitions for *cataclysm* and *catastrophe.* However, distinctions exist in the Greek roots of these words. The former can be defined as a "destructive washing down or inundation," such as the Biblical flood. *Catastrophe* [*kata + strephein,* "to turn," "to twist"] can mean "a sudden violent upheaval" such as an earthquake or, more generally, "a sudden calamity or complete failure," involving a sharp downward turn or twist. The catastrophe in classical tragedy is the twist of fate or crucial downward turn of events beyond which there is no recovery.

</td></tr>
</table>

7. catapult (kăt′ ə pŭlt′)   [*pallein* <G. "to toss," "to whirl"]
n. 1. An ancient mechanical device for hurling missiles.

From his research for the construction of an authentic **catapult**, the writer Jim Paul concluded that Alexander the Great "transformed western culture" through his shrewd and powerful use of this weapon.

2. A modern mechanism for launching aircraft from the deck of a ship.

Because flight decks on aircraft carriers are generally only 1,100 feet long, a **catapult** supplies the velocity planes need for take-off.

tr. and *intr. v.* To hurl or launch suddenly (as if from a slingshot); to spring up.

When Charles Lindbergh landed in Paris in 1927, becoming the first person to fly solo across the Atlantic Ocean, his flight **catapulted** him to international fame.

catapultic, *adj.*

SUB <L. "under"

Familiar Words
insubordinate
subjugate
submerge
subnormal
subordination
subsequent
subservient
subterranean
subvert
surreptitious

8. **subjective** (səb jĕk′ tĭv) [*jacere* <L. "to throw"] *adj.* 1. Concentrating on the self in the expression of feelings and perceptions.

Isadora Duncan's **subjective** interpretations of classical Greek dances were greatly admired in Europe but not in America.

2. Relating to personal opinions and thought processes rather than factual information or universal experience.

Readers of newspapers expect editorials and letters to the editors to express **subjective** views but news stories to contain verifiable, objective facts.

subjectivism, *n.*; **subjectivity**, *n.*
Antonym: **objective**

9. **sublimate** (sŭb′ lə māt) [*limen* <L. "threshold"] *tr.* and *intr. v.* To turn aside an instinctual, perhaps primitive, impulse in favor of a more socially or culturally acceptable activity.

Therapists attempt to train highly aggressive people to **sublimate** their impulses to fight by visualizing peaceable alternatives.

sublimate, *n.* and *adj.*; **sublimation**, *n.*

NOTA BENE: Although the word *sublimate* began as a psychological term, it is now in general usage. *Sublime*, "exalted" and "awe-inspiring," also contains elements of this meaning.

Challenge Words
subaltern
subaqueous
sub rosa
surrogate

10. **suborn** (sə bôrn′) [*ornare* <L. "to equip"] *tr. v.* 1. To induce a person in secret to commit a misdeed or a crime.

Mother Midnight **suborns** Moll Flanders by having her trained to pick pockets.

2. To induce someone to give false testimony.

When party members **suborned** the U.S. Secretary of the Interior, Albert B. Fall, to lie about the source of a loan for illegally leasing naval oil reserves, he became a central figure in the Teapot Dome scandal of the 1920s.

subornation, *n.*

11. **subterfuge** (sŭb′ tər fyōōj′)
[*fugere* <L. "to flee"]
n. An artifice, device, or evasion to hide or avoid something, or to escape an outcome.

After Kate Hardcastle learns that her suitor is too tongue-tied to speak with young women of his own social class, she adopts the **subterfuge** of appearing to be a family servant.

NOTA BENE: Under *sub* in any dictionary you will find from 100 to more than 500 words using the prefix, and many more with *sub* imbedded within words. For example, *surreptitious* comes from the Latin *subrepticus* meaning "snatched" (<L. *sub rapere* "to seize") and illustrates the hidden *sub*. As is the case in many English words, the transition from Latin to English forced *sub* to become *sur*, and slurred pronunciation eventually changed the spelling.

<table><tr><td>**Familiar Words**
veracious
veracity
verify
very</td></tr></table>

VERITAS <L. "truth"

12. **verisimilitude** (vĕr′ ə sĭm ĭl′ ə tōōd′, vĕr′ ə sĭm ĭl′ ə tyōōd′)
[*similis* <L. "of the same kind"]
n. A thing or a quality that appears true or real.

Critics cite John Edgar Wideman as a novelist who captures the speech and thought of urban African-American youth with **verisimilitude**.

13. **verity** (vĕr′ ə tē)
n. 1. The condition or quality of being true or accurate.

Scientists now accept as a **verity** that ninety-nine percent of all biological phenomena eventually become extinct.

2. A belief, principle, or statement expressing some basic human truth.

The writer must leave "no room in his workshop for anything but the old **verities** and truths of the heart, the old universal truths lacking which

<table>
<tr><td>

Challenge Words
verily
verism
veritas

</td></tr>
</table>

any story is ephemeral and doomed—love and honor and pity and pride and compassion and sacrifice."—William Faulkner

veritable, *adj*.

14. **aver**   (ə vûr′)   [I = ad <L. "to," "toward"]
    tr. v. To affirm; to declare or attest to positively or dogmatically.

After the Ancient Mariner's shipmates protest his killing of the albatross, he admits his error:
    And I had done a hellish thing,
    And it would work 'em woe:
    For all **averred**, I had killed the bird
    That made the breeze to blow.
          —Samuel Taylor Coleridge

averment, *n*.

NOTA BENE: Although *verity* and *veracity* look similar, they function differently; a scientific truth is a *verity*; we hope that scientists can be depended upon for their *veracity*, their capacity for telling the truth.

EXERCISE 6A

Circle the letter of the best SYNONYM for the word(s) in bold-faced type.

1. an imponderable **hypothesis**   a. conclusion   b. theory
     c. attitude   d. paradigm   e. deduction
2. **sublimating** a primitive impulse   a. hiding   b. remembering
     c. diverting   d. reproaching   e. refining
3. **catapulted** to the Baseball Hall of Fame   a. propelled   b. led
     c. voted   d. hurried   e. denied
4. chronic **hypochondria**   a. epicureanism   b. good health
     c. hyperventilation   d. invalidism   e. imaginery illness
5. **recumbent** Romans dining on couches   a. ascending
     b. reclining   c. standing   d. seated   e. relaxed
6. an eternal **verity**   a. similarity   b. archetype   c. levity
     d. falsehood   e. truth
7. **incumbent upon** all officials   a. the parameters of
     b. the duty of   c. the term of office of   d. the puissance of
     e. the demagoguery of
8. to **succumb to** flattery   a. resist   b. die of   c. induce
     d. suborn   e. acquiesce to
9. astonishing **verisimilitude**   a. falsity   b. repetition
     c. juxtaposition   d. dissimilarity   e. likeness

Circle the letter of the best ANTONYM for the word in bold-faced type.

10. an ingenious **subterfuge**   a. escape   b. subtlety   c. secrecy
    d. candor   e. contrivance
11. **averring** full responsibility   a. debasing   b. denying
    c. describing   d. reproaching   e. testifying to
12. **subjective** responses   a. grammatical   b. personal
    c. objective   d. irrelevant   e. critical

EXERCISE 6B   Circle the letter of the sentence in which the word in bold-faced type is used incorrectly.

1. a. The painting's brilliant but harsh colors and jagged shapes were said by some to **sublimate** the artist's anger.
    b. Experiments with subliminal advertising—brief exposure to a stimulus that develops a craving for a product before a person can consciously **sublimate** that impulse—have proved to be inconclusive.
    c. In letters to his nephew Wormwood, a neophyte devil, Screwtape recommends discouraging the **sublimation** of the lower instincts as a way to undermine the moral principles of the "patient."
    d. Harriet Doerr **sublimated** her writing talents for many years but fulfilled them at age seventy-four with her novel *Stones for Ibarra.*

2. a. Because children are natural mimics, their speech patterns and gestures in playing merchant or doctor have the **versimilitude** of adult mannerisms.
    b. Now that computers can reproduce the sounds of orchestral instruments with **verisimilitude**, composers can quickly hear and transcribe their compositions.
    c. When the second Mrs. Max de Winter appears at the fancy dress ball in a gown identical to one worn by Max's late wife, Rebecca, he and his guests are horrified by her **verisimilitude**.
    d. People who live in small apartments sometimes extend their view with a *trompe l'oeil* ("trick of the eye"), a painted screen or window shade of such **versimilitude** that people believe they are looking out a window.

3. a. Many people trusted the **verity** of the accused spies Ethel and Julius Rosenberg, but the defendants were convicted and executed for espionage in 1953.
    b. Although neutrons and protons are invisible, physicists accept them as a scientific **verity**.
    c. Edna Ferber acknowledges a **verity** in American attitudes when a character in *Cimarron* says, "I am not belittling the brave pioneer

men, but the sunbonnet as well as the sombrero has helped to settle this glorious land of ours."

    d. Athletes in competitive sports accept the **verity** that they can't win all the time.

4.   a. Thoughtful voters avoid evaluating candidates **subjectively** with responses like "I'm voting for Ms. X because she had surgery just like my mother's."

    b. The Paris diaries of Anaïs Nin record in **subjective** detail her relationships with writers and artists when she lived on a barge along the Seine.

    c. Geography textbooks contain **subjective** information about topography, climate, and population.

    d. An important aspect of romanticism is **subjectivity**, the emphasis on imagination and self-expression.

5.   a. If any of Hitler's bodyguards appeared to be disloyal, they could be **suborned** into illegal acts that would irrevocably tie them to criminality from which there was no escape.

    b. Boss Tweed of New York's Tammany Hall created such an echelon of political **subornation** that he and his henchmen were thirty million dollars richer before Tweed eventually went to prison on felony charges.

    c. Attempting to shatter the morale of American World War II troops in the Pacific, the soothing voice of Tokyo Rose **suborned** them to dream of home.

    d. A person going to trial may try to create an alibi by **suborning** friends and relatives to attest falsely.

6.   a. Masters of **subterfuge**, the lizards known as chameleons escape their enemies by changing color to blend with their surroundings.

    b. Shipwrecked and believing her twin brother dead, Viola adopts the **subterfuge** of male disguise and seeks employment in the house of Olivia.

    c. To forestall her suitors, Penelope says she must complete a funeral tapestry before she can marry, using the **subterfuge** of weaving by day and unraveling her work at night.

    d. In order to separate the cream from the milk, the farmer turned on the **subterfuge** at full speed.

7.   a. The Black Death, which raged through Asia and Europe from 1346 to 1361, resulted in a **cataclysm**: more than twenty-seven million people succumbed, leaving the survivors in a state of anarchy.

    b. In September 1938 the U.S. Weather Service failed to alert residents of the Northeast Coast to an imminent hurricane, a raging **cataclysmic** of winds and tides that caused vast destruction.

    c. A myth from British New Guinea tells that Radaulo, the king of snakes, saved the world from **cataclysmic** inundation by uncoiling itself from its mountain redoubt and using its fiery tongue to lick the waters back to their ocean bed.

d. The combination of Spanish guns and disease—smallpox, measles, and mumps—appears to have caused the **cataclysm** that reduced the population of twenty-five million Native Americans to one quarter of that number between 1518 and 1548.

EXERCISE 6C   Fill in each blank with the most appropriate word from Lesson 6. Use a word or any of its forms only once.

1. Argan, Molière's foolish _____, not only refuses to leave his bed and stop the prescribed purging, but he also tries to marry his daughter to a medical mountebank so that he will have a doctor in the family.

2. _____ that contaminated soil and groundwater are the deadly source of cholera rather than the bacillus itself, Dr. Max Pettenkofer proved his point in 1892 by swallowing a broth laden with germs and suffering no harmful aftereffects.

3. Maya Angelou _____ that "Hungry people cannot be good at learning or producing anything except perhaps violence."

4. When Gulliver awakens in Lilliput, he tries to rise from his

   _____ position but discovers "slender ligatures" tying him to the ground and feels forty small people advancing from his legs to his chest.

5. The popularity of Margaret Mitchell's *Gone with the Wind* helped

   the film adaptation _____ into the ranks of the most successful motion pictures ever made.

6. Richard M. Nixon, the second _____ president against whom impeachment proceedings were initiated, resigned from office in 1974.

7. After the Cincinnati Reds easily defeated the favored Chicago White Sox in the 1919 World Series, the public learned that

   professional gamblers had _____ eight White Sox players to lose the game for a promise of one hundred thousand dollars.

8. When Mount Vesuvius erupted in A.D. 79 and buried Pompeii and Herculaneum under ashes and cinders, the event seemed _____ to neighbors in the region, but

preservation of historical artifacts and architecture for more than 1500 years has justified its classification as catastrophic.

9.   In *Love in the Time of Cholera* Florentino Arizo _____ so completely to the charms of Fermina Daza that he is willing to wait fifty years to marry her.

EXERCISE 6D   Replace the word or phrase in italics with a key word or any of its forms from Lesson 6.

Human beings have endured many hardships wrought by the arbitrariness of nature and by human ignorance and intolerance. In the twentieth century, however, a different kind of terrible burden has emerged—a (1) *disaster on a huge scale* in the form of a nuclear holocaust. Helen Caldicott, an Australian physician, believes it to be (2) *essential to social responsibility* for citizens to discourage construction of nuclear arsenals, as she (3) *says with authority* in her book *Missile Envy: The Arms Race and Nuclear War*. Some novels (4) *offer a theory about* the destruction and change after a massive nuclear explosion. One of them, *A Canticle for Leibowitz* by Walter M. Miller, (5) *hurls* readers into a world portrayed with such (6) *apparently real qualities* that they feel only emptiness and desolation. Most living creatures have (7) *died*, genetic mutations have created monstrous deformities, and the planet is irrevocably altered. Literary speculations like this one remind readers of a paradox that is also a(n) (8) *basic human truth*: pursuit of goals that seem to have worthy ends can be destructive.

1. _____   5. _____

2. _____   6. _____

3. _____   7. _____

4. _____   8. _____

REVIEW EXERCISES FOR LESSONS 5 AND 6

1 Circle the letter of the best answer.

1. Which of the following words has no "up" in it?
   a. transcendent   b. echelon   c. preponderance   d. levitate
   e. escalate

2. Which of the following words has no "down" in it?
   a. cataclysm   b. succumb   c. debase   d. hypocrisy
   e. verisimilitude

3. Which is incorrect?
   a. under <L. *sub*
   b. below <L. *clivus*
   c. down <G. *kata*
   d. beneath <G. *hupo*
   e. low <L. *bassus*

4. leverage : weakness : :
   a. declivity : upward slope
   b. legerdemain : levity
   c. hypochondria : illness
   d. hypothesis : verity
   e. incumbency : transcendence

5. subjective : personal : :
   a. veritable : unverifiable
   b. ponderous : light
   c. imponderable : answerable
   d. suborning : false
   e. hypothetical : theoretical

6. *scandere* : *incumbere* : :
   a. to catapult : to sublimate
   b. to verify : to suborn
   c. to leaven : to hypothesize
   d. to ascend : to recline
   e. to levitate : to succumb

7. proclivity : tendency : :
   a. cataclysm : cyclone
   b. bas-relief : statue
   c. penchant : liking
   d. levity : gravity
   e. subterfuge : openness

2   Circle the letter of the most appropriate pair of words to complete the following sentences.

1. As they _____ the effect of the orbiting asteroids swarming in space, astronomers doubt that a(n) _____ will occur because large bodies explode upon entering the earth's atmosphere and small objects cause little damage.
   a. aver . . . debasement
   b. hypothesize . . . cataclysm
   c. sublimate . . . declivity
   d. preponderate . . . catapult
   e. levitate . . . verisimilitude

2. The _____ of martial figures on the monument in Tiananmen Square in Beijing demonstrates the _____ of nations to memorialize their military victories.
   a. echelon . . . verity
   b. levitation . . . subjectivity
   c. legerdemain . . . subterfuge
   d. bas-relief . . . proclivity
   e. preponderate . . . leverage

3. _____ for twenty years, Rip Van Winkle awakes to discover _____ changes in himself, his village, and his family.
   a. Hypocritical . . . leavening
   b. Incumbent . . . verisimiltudinous
   c. Succumbed . . . sublimated
   d. Ponderous . . . cataclysmic
   e. Recumbent . . . imponderable

3   Fill in each blank with the most appropriate word from Lessons 5 and 6. Use a word or any of its forms only once.

The earliest ballets were parts of operas, intervals of dance to separate

acts or to add a) _____ (frivolity) and movement

that could b) _____ (provide a lightening

influence to) the somewhat c) _____ (heavy,

weighty) operatic plot. Ballet later reached its high point at the court
of imperial Russia, which produced artists of the highest order.
Choreographers like Petipa, composers like Tchaikovsky and Stravinsky,
and dancers like Nijinsky and Pavlova combined talents to create

a(n) d) _____ (extraordinary, beyond normal

experience) art that still remains the standard for classical ballet.

However, the e) _____ (catastrophic) events of the Russian Revolution in 1917 drove many of these artists to Western Europe and North America, where they contributed to a revival of interest in ballet.

At the same time, however, a new genre was emerging, led by the American dancer Isadora Duncan. This so-called modern dance

emphasized natural movements and f) _____ (related to personal expressions) interpretations rather than the stylized and prescribed movements of classical ballet. Modern dancers preferred bare feet and simple draperies to the

g) _____ (artifice) of toe shoes and tutus.

Although at first traditionalists h) _____ed (declared dogmatically) that modern dance was only a

i) _____d (degraded) form of ballet. However, today, a century later, the two forms of dance have become complementary. Most dance companies perform both classical and modern compositions, and most dancers are trained in both styles.

4 Writing or Discussion Activities

1. Think about the way you might complete the following sentences. Then choose two of them to develop in separate paragraphs, citing a specific experience suggested by the italicized word; include appropriate colorful detail.
   a. It's easy for me to *succumb* to . . .
   b. I sometimes indulge in *subterfuge* when . . .
   c. I'm glad I was successful in *sublimating* . . .
   d. An *imponderable* question I sometimes ask is . . .
2. Apply your understanding of subjectivity and objectivity to a place that you know well and about which you have definite feelings, either positive or negative. You may use a family photograph of a house, a street, or a scene to give you ideas. Then write two paragraphs. Be objective in the first paragraph. Describe the place as factually as possible, giving visual details that are clear and straightforward, avoiding emotion. Be subjective in the second paragraph. Describe the place with vivid description and imagery to let a reader know your impressions and feelings about it.

Business

LESSON 7

Sumptus censum ne superet.
Let not your spending exceed your income
(i.e., Live within your means).—MARTIAL

Key Words		
acquisitive	importune	premise
demise	inquisition	presumption
dynamo	meretricious	querulous
dynasty	meritorious	subsume
emissary	opportunist	sumptuary

Familiar Words
conquer
exquisite
inquiry
prerequisite
quarrel
quest
question
require

QUAERO, QUAERERE, QUAESIVI, QUAESITUM <L. "to seek," "to search for"

1. **acquisitive** (ə kwĭz′ ə tĭv)
   [*ac* = *ad* <L. "to," "toward"]
   adj. Eagerly seeking to obtain things, wealth, or information.

   The astronomer Henrietta Leavitt, an **acquisitive** collector of data, discovered four novae and 2,400 variable stars and recognized the crucial relationship between stellar cycles and degrees of brightness.

   acquire, *v.*; **acquisition**, *n.*; **acquisitiveness**, *n.*

Challenge Words
disquisition
inquest
perquisite
query
requisition

2. **inquisition** (ĭn´ kwə zĭsh´ ən, ĭng´ kwə zĭsh´ ən)   [*in* <L. "in"]
n. 1. A prolonged inquiry or questioning, especially a harsh investigation on religious or political issues.

In 1952 when Lillian Hellman faced a government **inquisition** asking her to name people in the movie industry who might be Communists, she said, "I cannot and will not cut my conscience to fit this year's fashions."

2. (capitalized) The special court of the Roman Catholic church in the Middle Ages to combat, suppress, and punish heresy, i.e., any belief varying from orthodox doctrine.

In the belief that all scientific truth was contained in the Bible and the works of ancient Greek philosophers, the **Inquisition** suppressed all medical experimentation as heresy.

inquisitive, *adj.*; **inquisitor**, *n.*; **inquisitorial**, *adj.*

NOTA BENE: Although the Catholic church was the chief inquisitorial agency, a Protestant inquisition developed in the fifteenth century to combat elements in Catholic dogma. John Calvin in Geneva was especially harsh in persecuting those who questioned Protestant orthodoxy.

3. **querulous** (kwer´ yōō ləs)
adj. Complaining; irritable; peevish.

David Copperfield encounters Mrs. Gummidge, a **querulous** widow given to whimpering, "How could I expect to be wanted, being so lone and lorn, and so contrairy!"

querulousness, *n.*

Familiar Words
aerodynamics
dynamic
dynamite

DUNAMIS <G. "power"
DUNASTHAI <G. "to be able," "to have strength"

4. **dynamo** (dī´ nə mō)
n. 1. An electric generator.

In his autobiography, *The Education of Henry Adams*, the author cites two forces that epitomize the spiritual energy of their respective eras: the Virgin Mary in the Middle Ages and the **dynamo** in modern times.

2. An extremely forceful, energetic, or hardworking person.

A **dynamo** throughout his life, Thomas Edison experimented ceaselessly and collected patents for 1,093 inventions, among them the electric light, the phonograph, and the motion picture.

5. **dynasty** (dī′ nəs tē)
n. 1. A succession of rulers from the same family group or line.

The establishment of the Ming **dynasty** in 1368 brought a return to native hegemony in China after nearly a century of rule by Mongols.

2. A succession of influential people linked by familial, political, social, or cultural association.

The Redgrave theatrical **dynasty** comprises Michael Redgrave and Rachel Kempson, their offspring Vanessa, Corin, and Lynn, and their grandchildren.

dynastic, *adj.*; **dynastical**, *adj.*

MITTO, MITTERE, MISI, MISSUM <L. "to send"

6. **demise** (dĭ mīz′) [*de* <L. "away from"]
n. Death, or the end of existence or operation of something.

The practice of bloodletting with leeches, thought to be a cure-all, finally came to its **demise** in the 1850s when it proved to be either harmful or useless.

7. **emissary** (ĕm′ ĭ sĕr′ ē)
[*e* = *ex* <L. "from," "out of"]
n. A person sent on a special mission.

When John Alden, acting as an **emissary**, relays Miles Standish's marriage proposal to Priscilla Mullins, she asks, "Why don't you speak for yourself, John?"

8. **premise** (prĕm′ ĭs) [*pre* <L. "before"]
n. 1. A proposition offered as a basis for argument.

In Tony Hillerman's mystery stories the police officers Joe Leaphorn and Jim Chee base their **premises** of guilt or innocence on a deep understanding of Navajo culture.

2. In logic, each of the first two propositions in a syllogism.

In the syllogism, "All human beings die; I am a human being; therefore I shall die," the first two sentences are the major and the minor **premises**.

premise, *v.* (used only as a legal term)

NOTA BENE: The word *premises* can also mean "a building and its grounds"; for example, A visitor to San Simeon, the Hearst estate designed by Julia Morgan, may wander about the *premises*—the "castle," the terraces, and the extensive grounds overlooking the Pacific Ocean.

MEREO, MERERE, MERUI, MERITUM <L. "to earn," "to deserve," "to merit"

9. **meretricious** (měr´ ĭ trĭsh´ əs)
adj. 1. Attention-getting in a vulgar way; tawdry
or tacky.

When James Gatz in *The Great Gatsby* transforms
himself to Jay Gatsby at age seventeen, he becomes
committed to "the service of a vast, vulgar, and
meretricious beauty."

2. Insincere; based on pretense or deception.

The Better Business Bureau accepts complaints about **meretricious** car
repair: shoddy work, unnecessary repairs, or billing for repairs that
have not been made.

10. **meritorious** (měr´ ĭ tôr´ ē əs, měr´ ĭ tōr´ ē əs)
adj. Praiseworthy; deserving reward or esteem.

Barbara McClintock's **meritorious** contribution
to the understanding of DNA and "jumping" genes
earned her the Nobel Prize in physiology or
medicine in 1983.

PORTUS <L. "harbor," "gate"

11. **importune** (ĭm pôr tōōn´, ĭm pôr tyōōn´,
ĭm pôr´ chən) [*im = in* <L. "in"]
tr. v. To make repeated and insistent
demands or requests.

Describing to her father how Prince Hamlet
has been courting her, Ophelia declares,
"My lord, he hath **importuned** me with
love / In honourable fashion."

importunate, *adj.*; **importunity**, *n.*

12. **opportunist** (ŏp´ ər tōō´ nĭst, ŏp´ ər tyōō´ nĭst)
[*op = ob* <L. "off," "against"]
n. A person (or animal) taking advantage of any chance to achieve
an end in a forceful or self-serving way.

When trained dolphins are on display, they appear playful and gentle,
but in the wild they can become **opportunists**, attacking ruthlessly in
groups to test the power of potential mates or rivals.

opportunistic, *adj.*; **opportunistically**, *adv.*; **opportunism**, *n.*

Familiar Words
assume
consume
resume
sumptuous

Challenge Word
consumptive

SUMO, SUMERE, SUMPSI, SUMPTUM <L. "to take," "to obtain"

13. **presumption** (prĭ zŭm' shən)   [*pre* <L. "before"]
    n. 1. Arrogance; excessive self-assurance; unbecoming boldness.

    The Queen of Hearts intimidates the denizens of Wonderland by threatening to behead anyone who has the **presumption** to contradict her.

    2. Grounds for belief; assumption or supposition.

    The European **presumption** that Native Americans lacked "advanced culture" ignored their skill at resolving conflict by consensus of the whole community.

    presume, *v.*; **presumptive**, *adj.*; **presumptuous**, *adj.*;
    presumptuousness, *n.*

    NOTA BENE: Keep in mind that a presumption is not necessarily based on logical reasoning; it can be a whim and be entirely wrong. A premise is expected to undergo the test of logic or scientific evidence to determine its accuracy or truth.

14. **subsume** (səb sōōm', səb syōōm')   [*sub* <L. "under"]
    tr. v. To place in a larger category or under a general heading or principle.

    "Political buttons are **subsumed** under the larger collectors' category of ephemera, along with old theatre programs, menu cards from long-defunct ocean liners, and lobby posters advertising *Bulldog Drummond Returns*."—Gretchen Ackerman.*

    subsumption, *n.*

15. **sumptuary** (sŭmp' chōō ĕr´ ē)
    adj. Pertaining to or regulating expenditure, often for religious or moral reasons, usually relating to clothing or food.

    The letter *A* that Hester Prynne wears, "in fine red cloth, surrounded with an elaborate embroidery . . . was of a splendor in accordance with the taste of the age, but greatly beyond what was allowed by the **sumptuary** regulations of the colony."—Nathaniel Hawthorne

    NOTA BENE: The word *sumptuous*, although a relative of *sumptuary*, has an opposite meaning: "lavish; suggesting great expense or splendor."

---

*Quoted with permission from the author. "At the Sign of the Elephant and Donkey: Button-Hunting in New Hampshire," *The Walpole Gazette*, August 21, 1992.

EXERCISE 7A   Circle the letter of the best SYNONYM for the word in bold-faced type.

    1. a diplomatic **emissary**   a. businessperson   b. chaplain
        c. merchant   d. lecturer   e. go-between
    2. to **subsume** book titles   a. list   b. hypothesize   c. debase
        d. classify   e. renounce
    3. the **demise** of the U.S.S.R.   a. founding   b. end   c. descent
        d. ascent   e. failure
    4. a(n) **acquisitive** coin collector   a. curious   b. querulous
        c. clever   d. knowledgeable   e. grasping
    5. seizing the **opportune** moment   a. timely   b. ephemeral
        c. propinquitous   d. subjective   e. meritorious
    6. egregious **inquisitors**   a. annunciators   b. test makers
        c. demagogues   d. interrogators   e. respondents
    7. beginning with the **premise**   a. assumption   b. syllogism
        c. boldness   d. antithesis   e. archetype
    8. a powerful **dynamo**   a. fanatic   b. succession of rulers
        c. genius   d. engine   e. opportunist
    9. a(n) **importunate** class treasurer   a. impatient   b. meretricious
        c. opportunistic   d. hesitant   e. insistent
  10. a **meretricious** style of decoration   a. phony   b. quiescent
        c. garish   d. dignified   e. popular

Circle the letter of the best ANTONYM for the word in bold-faced type.

  11. unceasing **querulousness**   a. acquiescence   b. fretfulness
        c. cheerfulness   d. inquisitiveness   e. spitefulness
  12. a(n) **meritorious** performance   a. insincere   b. costly
        c. admirable   d. egregious   e. charitable
  13. an interloper's **presumptuousness**   a. timidity   b. gregariousness
        c. pomposity   d. slyness   e. smoothness

EXERCISE 7B   Circle the letter of the sentence in which the word in bold-faced type is used incorrectly.

    1. a. The death in 1991 of Rajiv Gandhi, the grandson of Jawaharlal
        Nehru and the son of Indira Gandhi, ended forty years of
        dynastic Nehru-Gandhi rule.
      b. The phrase "Virginia **dynasty**" refers to the regional origin
        of four of the first five U.S. presidents: George Washington,
        Thomas Jefferson, James Madison, and James Monroe.

    c. With the exception of two years when they lost the pennant, the New York Yankees' World Series **dynasty** lasted from 1949 to 1964.

    d. The noted Presbyterian minister Lyman Beecher **dynastied** thirteen children, one of whom was Harriet Beecher Stowe.

2. a. The Music Man, an opportunist with **meretricious** motives, convinces townspeople that buying his trombones will discourage their children from playing pool.

    b. In order to appear **meretricious** and well-read, some people fill their bookshelves with leatherbound pieces of wood and cardboard that look like the real thing.

    c. Proud and independent, Tatanka Iotanka, whom American settlers had the presumption to rename Sitting Bull, steadfastly refused to sign a treaty with agents of the U.S. government or to accept **meretricious** gifts he knew to be bribes.

    d. Writers who indulge in inappropriately ornate passages that trivialize the text are guilty of **meretriciousness** known as "purple prose."

3. a. All young Americans from infancy to adulthood are at some point **subsumed** under the term "kid."

    b. The genre of the mystery novel **subsumes** stories according to their protagonists, such as amateur sleuths, hard-boiled detectives, precinct police, spies, and historical figures.

    c. The term *folk art* **subsumes** a variety of forms and materials: primitive painting and sculpture, decoys, weathervanes, carousel animals, household tools, and baskets.

    d. In its fountains, gardens, and decorated archways, Segovia still **subsumes** the culture implanted during eight hundred years of Moorish presence in Spain.

4. a. Several Roman emperors attempted without success to enforce **sumptuary** control over the use of royal purple, which required costly dye from Tyre.

    b. During the English Regency, Queen Charlotte, mother of the Prince Regent, entertained more than 2,000 guests at a **sumptuary** garden party.

    c. When entering mosques or cemeteries in Muslim countries, visitors must adhere to **sumptuary** restrictions governing dress.

    d. The Roman emperor Diocletian's **sumptuary** *Edict on Maximum Prices* listed more than 1,000 items, including food, clothing, tools, and salaries of workers, artisans, and teachers.

5. a. As the emperor parades in new "clothes" woven with invisible thread by a pair of swindlers, the stunned crowd remains silent until a child has the **presumption** to say, "He doesn't have anything on!"

    b. By **presuming** that her destruction of Eilert Løvberg's manuscript is permanent, Hedda Gabler underestimates the power of Mrs. Elvsted to assist in its reconstruction.

    c. As heir **presumptive** to leadership of *The Washington Post,* Katharine Graham became president in 1963 and later publisher, encouraging aggressive investigative reporting of political and social issues.

    d. Excessive **presumption** of sweets leads to tooth decay.

EXERCISE 7C   Fill in each blank with the most appropriate word from Lesson 7. Use a word or any of its forms only once.

1. Oliver Goldsmith's Vicar of Wakefield observes, "When Sunday came, it was indeed a day of finery, which all

   of my _____ edicts could not restrain."

2. Contestants on television quiz programs must be intellectually

   _____ in order to summon answers to questions on a wide range of subjects.

3. Encouraged by Queen Isabella and King Ferdinand, the Grand

   Inquisitor of the Spanish _____, Tomás de Torquemada, had by 1492 accomplished the expulsion from Spain of 200,000 Jews who refused to convert to Catholicism.

4. Mary Wollstonecraft urged in her *Vindication of the Rights of Women* (1792) that girls and women be educated to become

   _____, able to earn a living in medicine, nursing, and business.

5. Formed in the 1980s, the Coalition for Women's Economic Development in Bangladesh functions on the

   _____ that small businesses can succeed with small loans if trust and cooperation are guaranteed.

6. In a sea battle against the Athenians, the Persian Artemisia

   _____ rammed another Persian vessel in order to save her own trireme.

7. Viewers grow weary of repetitive advertising that

   _____ them to acquire products and services.

8. While many American citizens of Japanese ancestry were egregiously incarcerated during World War II, Japanese-Americans

   were performing _____ military service at the same time.

9. Weary of his wife Zeena's _____ and nagging, Ethan Frome finds brief solace in the company of Mattie until a sledding accident makes invalids of them both.

10. For some stars of motion pictures the _____ of silent films meant the end of a career, but not for Lillian Gish, who continued performing in movies into the 1980s.

11. Participants in the Peace Corps, sharing expertise in teaching, health care, business, and other enterprises, have served as

American _____ to countries throughout the world.

12. Queen Elizabeth II of England continues the royal

_____ of the House of Windsor begun with King George V in 1910.

EXERCISE 7D   Replace the word or phrase in italics with a key word (or any of its forms) from Lesson 7.

According to official archives—manuals, checklists, and trial notes—religious (1) *interrogations, prolonged and harsh,* flourished intermittently in Europe from the twelfth to the nineteenth century. The (2) *reasoned basis* of the interrogations was that any failure to adhere to Christian doctrine threatened social order. However, at the same time, the clergy acted on their (3) *grounds for belief* that Satan and his demons existed and that witchcraft and sorcery were at work in what we now consider natural phenomena. The inquisitors could charge a defendant with various forms of witchcraft (4) *categorized* as divination, harmful magic, incantations and charms, and even healing.

(5) *Information-collecting* spies and informers pursued subjects, and (6) *insincere and deceptive* evidence could condemn a person. Inquisitors traveled from place to place to (7) *make insistent demands of* the accused to prove their innocence, confess their guilt, or recant. Resistance led to torture; those convicted of heresy or witchcraft were anathematized and put to death, often by being burned at the stake. The (8) *final days* of these inquisitions occurred in Spain in 1834.

1. _____   5. _____

2. _____   6. _____

3. _____   7. _____

4. _____   8. _____

LESSON 8

Caveat emptor.
Let the buyer beware.

Key Words

acerbic	comportment	plutocrat
acrid	exacerbate	preempt
acrimony	impecunious	purport
acumen	pecuniary	redemption
acute	peremptory	technocracy

Challenge Words
acerbate
acerose

ACER <L. "sharp"
ACERBO, ACERBARE, ACERBAVI, ACERBATUM
<L. "to make sour"
ACERBUS <L. "bitter," "sour," "harsh"

1. **acerbic** (ə sûrb′ ĭk) (also **acerb**)
   adj. 1. Sour or bitter in taste.

   Lemon, **acerbic** by itself, is refreshing when water and sugar turn it into lemonade.

   2. Harsh or sharp in speech, manner, or temper.

   Finding no assurance that her nephew is *not* engaged to Elizabeth Bennet, the **acerbic** Lady Catherine departs discourteously, sending "no compliments" to Mrs. Bennet.

   acerbity, *n.*

2. **acrid** (ak′ rĭd)
   adj. Bitterly pungent or harsh in taste or smell; sharply stinging.

   The **acrid** ammonia fumes in household cleansers can sting the eyes and constrict breathing.

   NOTA BENE: The word *acrid* can also be used to mean "stingingly sharp or caustic in language or tone," as in this acrid remark by I. F. Stone: "Every government is run by liars and nothing they say should be believed."

3. **exacerbate** (ĕg zăs′ ər bāt) [*ex* <L. "from," "out of"]
   tr. v. To increase the severity of something; to intensify irritation or violence.

   The relocation of highways and the construction of shopping malls have **exacerbated** the struggle of small town merchants to stay in business.

   exacerbation, *n.*

NOTA BENE: *Exacerbate* is a useful verb because it can serve as a synonym for both *aggravate* ("to heighten" anger, illness, or pain) and *irritate* ("to annoy" or "to provoke" a person) as in, Defeat can *exacerbate* an office-seeker. The latter usage, however, is less frequent than the former.

4. **acrimony** (ăk′ rə mō′ nē)
   n. Bitter, sharp animosity, especially in behavior or speech.

   Many women living under dictatorships where family members have disappeared sublimate their **acrimony** into active organizations such as Mothers of the Plaza de Mayo in Buenos Aires.

   acrimonious, *adj.*

Familiar Words
acid
acme

ACUO, ACUERE, ACUI, ACUTUM <L. "to sharpen"
ACUS <L. "needle"

5. **acumen** (ə kyōō′ mən)
   n. Keenness of insight and discernment; sagacity.

   Ramanujan, a mathematical genius from India, displayed his **acumen** by intuitive assumptions about the behavior of numbers that his colleagues found imponderable.

6. **acute** (ə kyōōt′)
   adj. 1. Very discerning; quickly alert to impressions.

   An **acute** observer and articulate advocate of the independence of Latin American countries, José Martí became known as the apostle of Cuban independence.

   2. Severe; intense.

   According to the biographer Elizabeth Longford, Annie Besant epitomized to an **acute** degree the Victorian woman coping with stress in courtship, marriage, motherhood, employment, politics, religion, and poverty.

   acuity, *n.*

Familiar Words
example
exemplify
impromptu
premium
prompt
prompter
pronto
sample

Challenge Word
irredentism

EMO, EMERE, EMI, EMPTUM <L. "to buy"

7. **peremptory** (pə rĕmp′ tə rē) [*per* <L. "through"]
adj. 1. Urgently commanding; officious or
arrogantly dictatorial.

In the French play *Chantecler*, the proud
cock, believing that the sun rises at his
bidding, says, "My song jets forth so clear,
so proud, so **peremptory** / That the horizon,
seized with a rosy trembling / Obeys me."

2. Not allowing contradiction or further disagreement.

Both civil and criminal courts grant lawyers for the defense and prose-
cution a specified number of **peremptory** challenges, the right to dismiss prospective jurors without giving a reason.

8. **preempt** (prē ĕmpt′) [*pre* <L. "before"]
tr. v. To take precedence over someone or something already
arranged or in place; to seize priority.

During the 1870s and 1880s, as two railroad barons vied to **preempt**
northwestern routes, Henry Villard first appeared the winner until James
Hill's greater financial acumen and stability prevailed.

9. **redemption** (rĭ dĕmp′ shən) [*re* <L. "back," "again"]
n. 1. Deliverance from sin; atonement for guilt.

Lord Jim finds **redemption** only when he accepts responsibility for a
death caused by his misjudgment.

2. Retrieval; reclamation; reformation.

Silas Marner must relinquish his greed for gold before his **redemption**
through love for little Eppie can occur.

redeem, *v.*; **redeemer**, *n.*; **redemptory**, *adj.*

NOTA BENE: *Redemption* (as an adjective or noun) meaning *reclamation*
also applies to the return of goods for cash: The 1972 Oregon Bottle
Refund Law encouraged the recycling of used containers at redemption centers.

KRATOS <G. "strength," "power"

10. **technocracy** (tĕk nŏk′ rə sē) [*tekhne* <G. "craft," "skill," "art"]
n. Government or social systems that put technological theories
into practice.

Familiar Words
aristocracy
autocrat
bureaucrat
democracy

Challenge Words
kakistocracy
meritocracy

Brave New World depicts a **technocracy** in which genetic engineering determines social organization: babies hatch from incubators according to a programmed caste system and are subjected to conditioning in communal nurseries.

technocrat, *n.*; **technocratic**, *adj.*

11. **plutocrat** (ploo′ tə krăt)
 n. A member of a governing wealthy class or a person whose wealth grants political influence.

 Strong leadership of the *New York Times* Company by three generations of the Ochs-Sulzberger dynasty brought the publishers professional distinction and made them **plutocrats**.

 NOTA BENE: Words ending in -*crat* are derived from *kratos* and indicate a partisan or member of a class type of government, as in *aristocrat* and *democrat*; the suffix -*cracy* identifies a type of government or authority, as in *autocracy* and *bureaucracy*.

Familiar Word
peculiar

Challenge Word
peculate

PECUNIA <L. "money," "wealth"*

12. **pecuniary** (pĭ kyoo′ nē ĕr´ ē)
 adj. Relating to money or necessary payment of it.

 Virginia Woolf addresses **pecuniary** concerns in *A Room of One's Own*: "A woman must have money and a room of her own if she is to write fiction."

 pecuniosity, *n.*; **pecunious**, *adj.*

13. **impecunious** (ĭm´ pĭ kyoo′ nē əs)
 adj. Lacking money; penniless.

 Living in São Paulo, Brazil, in the 1950s, Carolina Maria de Jesus kept a diary that records the daily lives of hopelessly **impecunious** neighbors who were nevertheless capable of humor and kindness.

 impecuniosity, *n.*

---

*Pecus <L. "cow." Cattle were a unit of exchange and therefore indicated wealth.

Familiar Words
deportation
deportment
export
import
importance
portable
portage
porter
portfolio
rapport
report
support
transport

Challenge Words
portamento
porterage
portmanteau

PORTO, PORTARE, PORTAVI, PORTATUM
<L. "to carry"

14. **comportment** (kəm pôrt′ mənt) [*cum* = <L. "with"]
n. Behavior; demeanor; mode of bearing or movement.

Although the "unsinkable" Molly Brown earned praise for her heroic action as the *Titanic* was sinking, she was notoriously meretricious in dress and **comportment**.

comport, *v.*

NOTA BENE: Dictionaries show that *comportment* and *deportment* can be synonyms. However, the former sometimes retains the connotation of "physical bearing": The speaker's *comportment* before a large audience indicated her experience in the theater. *Deportment* can be used to mean "conduct": Some schools give students grades for *deportment*.

15. **purport** (pər pôrt′, pər pōrt′) [*pur* = *pro* <L. "to forth"]
tr. v. To claim; to profess (without giving proof); to appear to be.

The builders **purported** the *Titanic* to be unsinkable, but on its maiden voyage to New York the ship struck an iceberg and sank.

purport, *n.*

EXERCISE 8A   Circle the letter of the best SYNONYM for the word in bold-faced type.

1. **pecuniary** legerdemain   a. epicurean   b. surprising
   c. monetary   d. cataclysmic   e. sumptuary
2. the **purported** discovery of ancient ruins   a. professed
   b. validated   c. renounced   d. unrequited   e. traduced
3. politic **comportment**   a. courtesy   b. comfort   c. habit
   d. agreement   e. demeanor
4. a(n) **acerbic** medicine   a. bitter   b. soothing   c. meretricious
   d. unpleasant   e. wholesome
5. to **redeem** a tarnished reputation   a. establish   b. retrieve
   c. interpose   d. induce   e. purport
6. a demagogue's **preemption**   a. withdrawal   b. purchase
   c. priority   d. disagreement   e. eviction
7. **acute** embarrassment   a. slight   b. endemic   c. puissant
   d. exacerbating   e. severe
8. **impecunious** during the Great Depression   a. unskilled
   b. impoverished   c. wealthy   d. employed   e. avaricious
9. a(n) **peremptory** tone   a. querulous   b. self-effacing
   c. dictatorial   d. opportunistic   e. reproachful

Circle the letter of the best ANTONYM for the word in bold-faced type.

10. the debater's **acrid** rebuttal   a. conciliatory   b. deft   c. harsh
    d. acriminious   e. offensive
11. the architect's **acumen**   a. brilliance   b. clarity   c. transcendence
    d. stupidity   e. sarcasm
12. **exacerbation** of the violence   a. deepening   b. analysis
    c. elimination   d. preemption   e. alleviation
13. **acrimonious** rivals   a. unrequited   b. friendly   c. opportunistic
    d. gregarious   e. antagonistic

EXERCISE 8B   Circle the letter of the sentence in which the word in bold-faced type is used incorrectly.

1. a. The presence of civilian **technocrats** and business investors in South Korea's authoritarian government in the 1980s helped to redistribute some wealth and encourage democratic processes.
   b. In his play *R.U.R.* (Rossum's Universal Robots), Karel Čapek satirizes a **technocracy** that frees people from tedious labor but also threatens human independence and purpose.
   c. Small businesses depend upon **technocratics** to handle advertising and bookkeeping.
   d. During the 1980s tension arose in Mexico between younger **technocrats** (*técnicos*) and older professional politicians (*politicos*).
2. a. When Clarissa Harlowe rejects a wealthy suitor she abhors, her **acrimonious** family disowns her, making her vulnerable to a relentless rake.
   b. *The Octopus* portrays the **acrimony** of midwestern wheat farmers exploited by railroad magnates and greedy grain speculators who control the price of grain.
   c. In *Brown Girl, Brownstones* Selina Brooks reacts with **acrimony** to stereotypical comments about servants and accents.
   d. Used in medicine, the bitter aloes plant has an **acrimonious** taste.
3. a. Sonia's **redemption** in *Crime and Punishment* occurs when a witness avers that she has not stolen the money discovered in her pocket.
   b. The U.S. Constitution protects citizens against **redemption**— being tried more than once for the same crime.
   c. Imprisoned for murdering her illegitimate child, Marguérite is nevertheless **redeemed** and ascends to heaven in Gounod's opera *Faust.*
   d. The Taos pueblo's **redemption** from the U.S. government of the sacred Blue Lake became a symbolic acknowledgment of Native American land rights.
4. a. The **plutocratic** Medici dynasty exerted not only political power as papal bankers but also cultural influence as patrons of the arts.

b. In 1895 a sociologist reasoned that **plutocrats'** wealth should benefit the economy rather than be unproductive in banks.

c. Asked to name a reward for his exceptional hospitality, King Midas chose **plutocracy**, the power to turn everything that he touched into gold.

d. Granting more power to the average worker in Japan after World War II required limiting the power of the **plutocracy**, or *zaibatsu*.

EXERCISE 8C   Fill in each blank with the most appropriate word from Lesson 8. Use a word or any of its forms only once.

1. In cases of national emergency—earthquakes, hurricanes, floods— television and radio broadcasters _____ scheduled programs with on-the-spot information.

2. Frank Thompson, a Union soldier exemplary in military _____ and performance of duty, was actually Sarah Emma Emmonds, who served for two years before illness caused her to desert in order to avoid detection.

3. Always quotable and usually _____, H. L. Mencken observed, "There are no dull subjects. There are only dull writers."

4. Victoria Ocampo's literary _____ enabled her to translate and publish the works of writers from South America, North America, and Europe in her magazine, *Sur.*

5. The Kwakiutl people of the Northwest acquire power from becoming _____ when they ceremoniously give away their prized possessions in the ritual of potlatch.

6. _____ because another officer wins the promotion he desires, Iago takes revenge by undermining Othello's faith in his wife, Desdemona.

7. When motorists hear the _____ siren of an approaching emergency vehicle, they should slow down and stop in the right-hand lane.

8. The _____ smell that lingers after a major fire dissipates slowly.

9. Although the overseers of the dam at the South Fork Reservoir above Johnstown, Pennsylvania, _____ it to be secure, inadequate repair and heavy rains in 1889 sent water raging down the valley with a cost of two thousand lives.

10. By marrying Khadija, a wealthy widow, the impecunious Muhammad gained a fortune, a faithful convert, and access to the _____ society of traders in Mecca.

11. Robert Frost contemplates _____ matters in these lines: "Never ask of money spent / Where the spender thinks it went."

12. A(n) _____ attempts to find a solution to satisfy a particular need without necessarily being concerned with its social, material, or moral implications.

13. Using archival data and the latest technology, scientists have

    determined that solar energy has _____ the continuing tilt of the leaning tower of Pisa.

14. The andromeda strain carried by a contaminated satellite sends

    the population into a(n) _____ panic, but four technocrats control the lethal organism and avert a national catastrophe.

EXERCISE 8D   Replace the word or phrase in italics with a key word (or any of its forms) from Lesson 8.

The forerunner of the automobile, a Chinese steam-powered cart, appeared in the ninth century B.C. Developments in Europe in the eighteenth and nineteenth centuries climaxed as the internal combustion engine using gasoline (1) *took precedence over* steam, coal-gas, and electricity as a source of power. Between 1886 and 1906 cars with the eponymous names of Benz, Daimler, and Rolls-Royce were excellently constructed and luxurious, but only (2) *members of the wealthy class* were affluent enough to buy them. Believing that cars ought to be affordable for workers, Henry Ford used his mechanical and business (3) *insight* to invent the assembly line that enabled the Ford Motor Company to mass-produce fifteen million inexpensive cars between 1908 and 1927.

After World War II, a similar development from larger to smaller and more economical cars took place. At first, companies led by (4) *people relying on technology* catered to the (5) *seeming* preference of American buyers for large gas guzzlers. In the 1950s, however, smaller fuel-efficient imports from Japan and Germany challenged the American market. A(n) (6) *severe* shortage of oil in 1973 (7) *increased the severity of* this threat, forcing (8) *arrogantly dictatorial* American manufacturers to acquiesce to the economic logic of smaller automobiles.

1. _____   5. _____

2. _____   6. _____

3. _____   7. _____

4. _____   8. _____

REVIEW EXERCISES FOR LESSONS 7 AND 8

1 Circle the letter of the best answer.

1. Which of the following words has no "sharpness" in it?
    a. exacerbate   b. acute   c. acquisitive   d. acrid
    e. acumen
2. Which of the following words has no "earning" or "buying" in it?
    a. redemption   b. meritorious   c. preempt   d. inquisition
    e. meretricious
3. querulous : *quaerere* : :
    a. meretricious : *emere*   d. inquisitive : *mittere*
    b. opportunistic : *portare*   e. peremptory : *merere*
    c. sumptuary : *sumere*
4. acumen : acute : :
    a. demise : dynastic   d. acrimony : querulous
    b. redemption : subsumed   e. acerbity : acrid
    c. plutocracy : pecuniary
5. *dunasthai* : *kratos* : :
    a. *acer* : *acuere*   d. *portare* : *portus*
    b. to have strength : strength   e. to send : emissary
    c. dynasty : technocracy

2 Matching: On the line at the left, write the letter of the statement that best matches the numbered pair of words.

_____ **1.** pecuniary   _____ **5.** meritorious dynasty
            redemption
                                  _____ **6.** acrimonious emissary
_____ **2.** meretricious
            plutocrat   _____ **7.** impecunious technocrat

_____ **3.** importuned dynamo _____ **8.** exacerbating preemption

_____ **4.** querulous   _____ **9.** sumptuary presumption
            opportunist
                                  _____ **10.** acerbic inquisitor

A. In college I plan to major in physics and engineering and get
    elected to public office quickly; it'll be hard though because I
    haven't a penny to pay for it.
B. It wasn't enough that a couple got ahead of me in line at the movies,
    but they also tried to sneak in without paying.
C. I'm the fourth generation of famous cooks, and every one of us has
    won a major culinary award.
D. I'm celebrating! I finally have the money I need to redeem the gui-
    tar I pawned.
E. I try to get my share or more at every chance, and when I don't,
    I fret.

F. As a member of the student court I like questioning the witnesses,
    but my acrid humor sometimes gets out of hand.
G. OK, I'm a showoff, but I just happen to like flashy clothes, and since
    I have a lot of money to spend, why not?
H. I have so much acuity and energy that people are always making
    demands, wanting me to be on committees.
I. When I attended the city council meeting to plead for a recreation
    center for teenagers, the negative response made me bitter.
J. Since I knew you were on a strict diet and couldn't eat that rich
    dessert, I ate it for you.

3   Fill in each blank with the most appropriate word from Lessons 7 and 8.
Use a word or any of its forms only once.

In the late 19th century, a new class of American

a) _____s (members of a wealthy class) arose,

self-made b) _____s (energetic, hardworking
persons) from the Midwest and West who achieved great wealth

through their business c) _____ (keen

discernment), d) _____ (practice of taking
forceful advantage), and good luck.

However, their e) _____ (financial) success was
usually in acute contrast to their lack of sophistication and education.

f) _____ (Eagerness to obtain) for the culture
they lacked drew many to New York and Europe, where novelists of

the time satirized their g) _____ (vulgar,

attention-getting) h) _____ (behavior) and their

i) _____ (pertaining to spending) excesses. For
example, in *The Custom of the Country*, Edith Wharton charts the career
of Undine Spragg, a presumptuous heiress who comes to New York
from "Apex City"; in *The House of Mirth* she depicts the newly rich Mrs.

Sam Gormer, who hires a(n) j) _____
(impoverished) socialite to teach her manners and help her break into
New York society.

4 Writing or Discussion Activities

1. Choose one of the words below that reminds you of a recent incident that you experienced yourself or observed. Write a paragraph describing the circumstances, the action involved, and the effect of that action.

acerb	dynamic	meritorious
acquisitive	exacerbating	opportunistic
acrimonious	impecunious	peremptory
acute	inquisitive	querulous

2. From a novel, short story, play, or poem that you have read recently, choose a character who in some specific action or trait illustrates the meaning of one of the words above. Provide a specific context or setting to make your point clear.

LESSON 9

Light and Dark

LESSON 9

Lux et veritas.
Light and truth.—Motto of Yale University

Key Words		
adumbrate	luminary	palliate
denigrate	luminescence	pallid
elucidate	muster	pellucid
lucent	necromancy	remonstrate
lucid	pall	umbrage

Familiar Words
Lucille
Lucinda
Lucy
translucent

LUCEO, LUCERE, LUXI, LUCTUM <L. "to shine"
LUX, LUCIS <L. "light"

1. **lucent**   (lōō′ sənt)
   adj. 1. Shining; luminous.

   In 1925 the astronomer Edwin Hubble demonstrated that the Andromeda nebula, a distant "cloudy" mass of **lucent** bodies, is a galaxy far outside this galaxy.

   2. Permitting light to pass through; translucent.

   Lacking glass, early pioneers in the Appalachian Mountains used **lucent** sheets of mica for the windows of log cabins.

82

2. **lucid**   (lōō' sĭd)
   adj. 1. Clearly expressed; easy to understand.

   Rachel Carson's **lucid** arguments about the environmental dangers of DDT eventually led to legislation controlling its use.

   2. Logical; rational; sane.

   Francis Bacon wrote that although the madness of King Henry VII of England usually caused him to rave, he also had "**lucid** intervals and happy pauses."

   lucidity, *n.*

3. **elucidate**   (ĭ lōō' sə dāt´)   [*e = ex* <L. "from," "out of"]
   tr. v. To make clear or plain; to clarify.

   Malinche, a captive Aztec woman who **elucidated** the complexities of local political rivalries for Cortez and his small Spanish army, helped them make allies and ultimately conquer the Aztec nation.

   elucidation, *n.*; **elucidative**, *adj.*; **elucidator**, *n.*

4. **pellucid**   (pə lōō' sĭd)   [*pel = per* <L. "through"]
   adj. 1. Very clear, thus allowing a maximum of light to pass through; transparent; translucent.

   The outer cell membrane of a cell is **pellucid**, permitting all interior structures to be clearly visible under a microscope.

   2. Very clear in meaning or style.

   Virginia Woolf's **pellucid** essays reflect her father's advice "to write in the fewest words, as clearly as possible, exactly what one meant."

   pellucidity, *n.*; **pellucidness**, *n.*

LUMENS, LUMENIS <L. "light"

5. **luminary**   (lōō' mə nĕr´ ē)
   n. 1. An object, such as the sun or moon, that gives light.

   Using the movement of **luminaries** like the planets, the ancient Maya developed a calendar so sophisticated that its predictions of the risings and eclipses of Venus have had only a two-hour margin of error in nearly five hundred years.

2. A person who is outstanding in a particular field.

Babe Didrikson Zaharias, a sports **luminary** in basketball, track and field, and golf, won more medals and dominated more sports than any other athlete of the twentieth century.

6. **luminescence**   (lōō′ mə něs′ əns)   [*crescere* <L. "to grow," "to increase"]
n. Light emitted by means other than burning, such as chemical or biochemical action or radiation.

A **luminescence** called corona discharge or Saint Elmo's fire occurs when the mast of a ship serves as a conducting surface and causes the surrounding atmosphere to ionize and glow.

luminescence, *v.*; **luminescent**, *adj.*

NOTA BENE: Many familiar words and trade names derive from the Greek roots *phos* and *photos*, meaning "light." Here, for example, are a few of the many words derived from *photos* that refer to light.

photoactive	photoengraving	photophilic
photobiotic	photokinesis	photophobia
photochemistry	photometer	photosynthesis
photoelectric	photonuclear	phototherapy

Since the invention of photography in the nineteenth century, a number of new words derived from *photos* that refer specifically to photography have entered the English language.

photocopy	photogravure	photomontage
photo finish	photoheliographic	photo-offset
photogenic	photojournalism	photoplay
photograph	photolithograph	photostat

MONSTRO, MONSTRARE, MONSTRAVI, MONSTRATUM <L. "to point out," "to show"

7. **muster**   (mŭs′ tər)
tr. v. 1. To assemble people, especially troops, for a specific purpose.

When the Romans invaded her territory, Queen Boadicea **mustered** the Britons and decimated a Roman legion before she was ultimately defeated.

2. To gather; to summon (often used with *up*).

Because he cannot **muster up** the courage to express his love, Cyrano de Bergerac must let another speak to Roxane the passionate words that he himself supplies.

NOTA BENE: The military use of *muster* has led to several interesting words and phrases. For example, the phrase *to pass muster*, meaning "to measure up to a certain standard," is derived from the former legal obligation of all American men to present themselves on a designated *muster day* to be registered for potential military service. Those found unfit for war did not *pass muster* while the able-bodied were entered into the *muster roll*, a roster of members in a military unit. These registered men might then expect in times of war to be *mustered in*, or enlisted, and at the end of their service, they were *mustered out* to rejoin civilian life.

8. **remonstrate** (rĭ mŏn′ strāt′)
[*re* <L. "back," "again"]
intr. v. To speak in protest or disapproval (often used with *with* or *against*).

After seeing three children killed in cross fire on the streets of Belfast, Betty Williams began to **remonstrate** against the violence and to organize a peace movement among women in Northern Ireland.

remonstration, *n.*; **remonstrative**, *adj.*; **remonstrator**, *n.*

Familiar Words
somber
sombrero
umbrella

Challenge Words
penumbra
umbra

UMBRA <L. "shade," "shadow"

9. **umbrage** (ŭm′ brĭj)
n. Extreme offense; resentment (usually with *take*).

Most natives of Scotland take **umbrage** at being called Scotch; they refer to themselves as Scots.

10. **adumbrate** (ăd′ əm brāt′, ə dŭm′ brāt) [*ad* <L. "to," "toward"]
tr. v. 1. To give a sketchy outline.

Since your textbook describes the building of the Panama Canal in full detail, today's lecture will only **adumbrate** the topic.

2. To foreshadow indistinctly.

Kristallnacht, a night in 1938 when Nazis attacked many German Jewish businesses and places of worship, **adumbrated** the Holocaust that was to come during World War II.

adumbration, *n.*

Challenge Word
niello

NIGER <L. "black," "dark-colored"

11. **denigrate**   (dĕn' ĭ grāt)   [*de* <L. "away from"]
tr. v. To speak derogatively of someone's character or reputation;
to defame; to disparage.

"Unfortunately [modern feminists] did not anticipate that *liberation*
would be caricatured as 'lib,' 'libbie,' and 'libbest' and thus used to
denigrate the women's movement."—Jo Freeman

denigration, *n.*; **denigrative**, *adj.*; **denigrator**, *n.*

12. **necromancy**   (nĕk' rə măn´ sē)
[*manteia* <G. "divination"]
n. 1. The art of predicting events by allegedly
communicating with the dead.

The three "weird sisters" use **necromancy** to call up
the spirit of Banquo, who holds a mirror that shows
a long line of kings descending from him.

2. Black magic; witchcraft; sorcery.

During the summer of 1692 in Salem, Massachusetts,
nineteen people who had been accused and convicted
of **necromancy** of were put to death.

necromancer, *n.*; **necromantic**, *ad.*;
necromantical, *adj.*

NOTA BENE: *Necromancy* evolved from a confusion of two similar
words combined with the Greek word *manteia*, meaning "divination." The medieval Latin word *nigromantia* used the Latin word
niger, "black," and meant "black magic." The Greek word *nekromteia*
used the word *necros*, meaning "corpse"; *nekromteia* was an ancient
method of divination in which the spirits of the dead were summoned and consulted about future events. The contemporary word
necromancy combines the ideas of both magic and communication
with the dead.

Familiar Words
appall
pale
pallor

PALLO, PALLERE, PALLUI, PALLETUM <L. "to be pale," "to long for"

13. **pall**   (pôl)
n. 1. A cover for a coffin or tomb.

The American flag may be used as a **pall** to cover the casket of someone who has served in the U.S. military.

2. A coffin, especially one with a body in it.

The **pall** of Martin Luther King, Jr., was carried through the streets of Atlanta on a simple wagon drawn by mules.

3. Anything that covers, darkens, obscures, or makes gloomy.

The 1883 eruption of a volcano on the Indonesian island of Krakatoa released a **pall** of pumice and dust that rose twenty miles into the stratosphere and was carried almost around the world.

intr. v. To become dull, tiresome, or lifeless.

The hula hoop was an overnight sensation, but not surprisingly, the fad for swinging a plastic circle around the hips quickly **palled**.

14. **palliate** (păl′ ē ăt)
tr. v. 1. To make a situation, especially an offense, seem less serious; to make excuses for something or someone.

Conclusive evidence that the accused acted in self-defense **palliated** the crime and resulted in murder charges being reduced to manslaughter.

2. To make less severe; to alleviate.

According to Katherine Mansfield, time has power to **palliate** sufferings: "As in the physical world, so in the spiritual world, pain does not last forever."

palliation, *n.*; **palliative**, *adj.*

15. **pallid** (păl′ ĭd)
adj. Deficient in color; having an abnormally pale complexion.

Unlike mountaineers, who are tanned by sun and wind at high altitudes, spelunkers, who explore caves, usually emerge quite **pallid** from long expeditions underground.

2. Lacking color, vitality, or interest; dull.

While they live out their **pallid** lives in a provincial Russian town, the three sisters dream of someday moving to Moscow.

pallidness, *n.*

EXERCISE 9A

Circle the letter of the best SYNONYM for the word(s) in bold-faced type.

1. a pool of **pellucid** water   a. rational   b. polluted   c. lukewarm   d. clear   e. conducive

2. Don't take **umbrage**.   a. abuse   b. a break   c. it lightly
    d. offense   e. the chance
3. **adumbrated** by recent events   a. overwhelmed   b. downcast
    c. confused   d. presaged   e. clarified
4. to **muster** enthusiasm   a. suppress   b. interdict   c. arouse
    d. redound with   e. disperse
5. a surprising **luminescence**   a. elucidation   b. deduction
    c. altercation   d. radiation-induced light   e. light from a coal fire
6. a(n) **lucent** being   a. clear-headed   b. imaginary   c. sumptuary
    d. puissant   e. radiant
7. the **elucidation** of a problem   a. cause of   b. exegesis of
    c. remonstrance against   d. palliation of   e. solution to
8. the **denigration** of modern art   a. belittling   b. praise   c. unity
    d. exclusiveness   e. altruism
9. to speak **lucidly**   a. wittily   b. acrimoniously   c. logically
    d. gracefully   e. briefly

Circle the letter of the best ANTONYM for the word(s) in bold-faced
type.

10. a **pallid** visage   a. sickly   b. vivid   c. debased   d. lucent
    e. pellucid
11. a real **luminary**   a. plutocrat   b. bon vivant   c. conjurer
    d. joke   e. nobody
12. a(n) **palliation of** the shock   a. numbing of   b. subsuming of
    c. depreciation of   d. intensification   e. adjustment to
13. to speak **remonstratively**   a. depreciatively   b. reproachfully
    c. altruistically   d. in parables   e. approvingly

EXERCISE 9B   Circle the letter of the sentence in which the word in bold-faced type is
used incorrectly.

1. a. The **pall** of polluted air that usually hangs over Athens is a threat
        not only to its citizens but also to its ancient monuments.
    b. Thousands of mourners filed solemnly past the **pall** of their
        revered leader.
    c. Low energy, brittle fingernails, and a distinct **pall** are some of the
        symptoms of anemia.
    d. Eustacia Vye's interest in Clym Yeobright **palls** when she realizes
        that he does not intend to return to Paris but to settle on
        desolate Egdon Heath.

2.   a. Millions of **luminaries** that can be seen with a telescope are invisible to the naked eye.
     b. Popular in the 1960s, the lava lamp has now become a classic of **luminary** bad taste.
     c. Some **luminaries**, like stars, shine with their own incandescence; others, like the moon, are lucent from reflected light.
     d. Many artistic **lumininaries** such as Zora Neale Hurston, Countee Cullen, and Langston Hughes lived and worked in Harlem in the 1920s, a period now known as the Harlem Renaissance.

3.   a. Critics praise the poetry of Mary Oliver as both **lucid** and lyrical.
     b. During the early stages of Alzheimer's disease a patient may alternate between periods of **lucidity** and periods of severe memory loss.
     c. Because of Medea's seemingly **lucid** behavior, no one except her old nurse suspects that she is about to commit murder.
     d. People on earth see only the lower levels of the aurora borealis's **lucid** display, which takes place from forty to six hundred miles above the earth.

4.   a. Although she commented in detail on comportment in the imperial court, Lady Muraski only **adumbrated** the underlying political tensions.
     b. Christian critics who idolized the Roman poet Virgil interpreted many of his passages as **adumbrations** of the coming of Jesus.
     c. The novel Jane Austen wrote as a teenager **adumbrates** her gift for social satire, but its title, *Love and Freindship*, betrays a weakness in her spelling.
     d. **Adumbrated** by the shadow of the Matterhorn, winter snows persist in villages on the north side of the mountain.

5.   a. The plot of a **necromantic** novel is predictable: boy and girl meet, fall in love, marry, and live happily after.
     b. Among some native peoples of Brazil, a shaman conducts **necromantic** rites to seek the advice of ancestors.
     c. Desperate to learn his future, King Saul resorts to **necromancy**, commanding the Witch of Endor to raise the spirit of the prophet Samuel from the dead.
     d. Although feared by some as a **necromancer**, Dona Ultima is shown to be a benign healer in the novel *Bless Me, Ultima*.

6.   a. During the Civil War each county of the Confederacy **mustered** its own troops; since neighbors often fought side by side, the young men of a district could be decimated in a single battle.
     b. **Mustering** my determination, I told my supervisor that I deserved a raise.
     c. Research shows that the average preschool child **musters** more than twenty hours per week watching television.
     d. Although you are passing all your subjects, your grades do not pass **muster** for college admission.

EXERCISE 9C   Fill in each blank with the most appropriate word from Lesson 9. Use a
                     word or any of its forms only once.

1. The _____ that made the legendary Hound
   of the Baskervilles so terrifying resulted from phosphorescent
   paint.

2. Although the publication of *Jane Eyre* in 1847 brought Charlotte
   Brontë acclaim after years of obscurity, the deaths of her brother

   and sisters in the next two years cast a(n) _____
   over her success.

3. Their white hands and _____ complexions
   distinguished well-born nineteenth-century European "ladies"
   from laboring women who could not protect themselves from
   the sun.

4. Roman emperors were said to have _____
   the discontent of the plebeians with "bread and circuses," cheap
   food and flamboyant public entertainments.

5. Although the spectacle of traditional Japanese Noh theater is

   impressive, most foreigners need some _____
   to appreciate the subtleties of the action.

6. Because the royal family of Nepal is considered divine, to

   _____ its members publicly is considered a
   sacrilege.

7. Having served a prison term for opposition to World War I, Kate

   Richards O'Hare spent the rest of her life _____
   with officials over the poor conditions in America's penitentiaries.

8. Although glass is heavy and expensive, most artists prefer it

   to plastic for framing because it is more _____
   and does not distort color.

9. Many people with disabilities take _____ at
   being called *handicapped* because the word suggests someone
   begging for a donation "with cap in hand."

10. Alonso of Aragon was described as "a great _____,
    for that he used to ask counsel of the dead," meaning that as a
    scholar, he consulted many books.

11. In *Paradise Lost* John Milton describes the sun as ". . . the great

    _____, . . . / That from his lordly eye
    keeps distance due, / Dispenses light from far."

EXERCISE 9D   Replace the word or phrase in italics with a key word (or any of its forms) from Lesson 9.

Until modern science could (1) *clarify* the sources of (2) *light produced by means other than burning*, this mysterious glow was the subject of much fearful folklore. A principal source of this light is the energy released by certain fungi in decaying wood, usually found in marshy places. Known in English as will-o'-the-wisp, foxfire, or friar's lantern (in Latin, *ignis fatuus*, or "fool's fire"), this glow often led travelers astray if they (3) *summoned* up the courage to pursue it. Because this light seemed to flit about in remote places and often appeared in colors of (4) *shining* red, yellow, blue, or green, it was also called witches' fire and associated with (5) *black magic*.

1. _____   4. _____

2. _____   5. _____

3. _____

LESSON 10

Open and Shut

LESSON 10

Numerus clausus.
A closed number (a quota that excludes all but a few).

Key Words

apocalypse	chasten	diaspora
apocryphal	clavier	diatribe
apoplexy	conclave	enclave
apostate	diadem	occlusion
castigate	diametrical	recluse

APO <G. "away from"

1. **apocalypse** (ə pŏk′ ə lĭps′)
   [*kaluptein* <G. "to cover"]
   n. 1. A prophetic disclosure or revelation, especially concerning a universal cataclysm.

   Old Norse literature describes the **apocalypse** known as Ragnarok, the ultimate battle with the powers of evil that will destroy both the divine and mortal worlds.

   2. Any widespread destruction.

   The anarchic regime of Pol Pot and his Khmer Rouge militia, who ruled Cambodia in the 1970s, created an **apocalypse** that destroyed the country's economy and took the lives of at least three million Cambodians.

Challenge Words
apocatastasis
apocope
apodictic
apodosis
apologue
apothegm

3. (capitalized) The last book of the Bible, also known as Revelation, which contains prophesies about the ultimate destruction of the world.

The most famous of Albrecht Dürer's woodcuts depicting scenes from the **Apocalypse** shows the Four Horsemen of the **Apocalypse**—Pestilence, Famine, War, and Death—spreading destruction as they ride across the earth.

apocalyptic, *adj.*; **apocalyptical**, *adj.*; **apocalypticism**, *n.*; **apocalyptist**, *n.*

2. **apocryphal**   (ə pŏk′ rə fəl)   [*kruptein* <G. "to hide"]
adj. False; counterfeit; doubtful, especially in authorship or authenticity.

According to Sir Isaac Newton, the idea for his theory of gravity came to him when he saw an apple fall, but the story that the apple fell on his head is surely **apocryphal**.

apocrypha, *n.*; **Apocrypha**, *n.*

NOTA BENE: Used with a capital letter, *Apocryphal* and *Apocrypha* refer specifically to fourteen ancient texts whose inclusion in the Bible is a topic of disagreement. Although included in Bibles authorized by the Roman Catholic Church, these books are generally omitted from Protestant Bibles on the grounds that they are not included in ancient Hebrew texts.

3. **apoplexy**   (ăp′ ə plĕk′ sē)   [*plessein* <G. "to strike"]
n. A stroke; a sudden loss of muscular control, sensation, or consciousness usually resulting from rupture or blockage of a blood vessel (often used hyperbolically to describe a state of extreme rage that produces exaggerated responses).

Mary Todd Lincoln, the president's wife, suffered attacks of **apoplexy** during which she would writhe, foam at the mouth, and lose consciousness.

apoplectic, *adj.*

4. **apostate**   (ə pŏs′ tāt, ə pŏs′ tĭt)   [*histanai* <G. "to stand"]
n. A person who forsakes his or her own principles, religion, or allegiances.

A longtime Democrat, Senator Strom Thurmond of South Carolina became a political **apostate** in 1964 when he joined the Republican party.

apostasy, *n.*; **apostate**, *adj.*; **apostatize**, *v.*

Familiar Words
caste
chaste
chastise
chastity

CASTUS <L. "pure," "spotless"
CASTIGO, CASTIGARE, CASTIGAVI, CASTIGATUM
<L. "to punish," "to correct," "to restrain"

5. **castigate** (kăs′ tə gāt)
[*agere* <L. "to do," "to make"]
tr. v. To punish; to criticize severely;
to chastise.

In the most famous of his "Orations against
Catiline," Cicero **castigated** the senator for
his treachery: "How long, O Catiline, will
you abuse our patience?"

castigation, *n.*; **castigator**, *n.*; **castigatory**, *adj.*

6. **chasten** (chā′ sən)
tr. v. To seek to improve through punishment; to discipline.

. . . I have learned
To look on nature, not as in the hour
Of thoughtless youth; but hearing often-times
The still, sad music of humanity,
Nor harsh, nor grating, though of ample power
To **chasten** and subdue.—William Wordsworth

chastened, *adj.*; **chastener**, *n.*

Familiar Words
claustrophobia
close
cloister
closet
closure
conclude
disclose
enclose
exclude
include
preclude

CLAUDO, CLAUDERE, CLAUSI, CLAUSUM <L. "to close"

7. **occlusion** (ə klōō′ zhən)   [*oc* = *ob* <L. "off," "against"]
n. Something that blocks; an obstruction.

Dr. Helen Taussig helped to develop a surgical correction to save "blue
babies," many of whom are born with an **occlusion** of the artery linking
the heart and lungs.

occlude, *v.*; **occludent**, *adj.*; **occlusive**, *adj.*

8. **recluse** (rĕk′ lōōs, rĭ klōōs′)   [*re* <L. "back," "again"]
n. Someone who lives alone and avoids company; a hermit.

Exiled from court, Anne Finch, Countess of Winchilsea, lived as a **recluse**
at her country home, where "the solitude and security of the country"
inspired her nature poetry.

reclusion, *n.*; **reclusive**, *adj.*

Challenge Words
cloisonné
foreclose

Familiar Words
clavicle
clef

CLAVIS <L. "key"

9. clavier (klə vîr′, klā′ vē ər, klăv′ ē ər)
n. A keyboard instrument, like a piano or
harpsichord, with strings.

J. S. Bach is said to have preferred the
sweet, quiet sound of the clavichord,
an early form of **clavier**, to any other
keyboard instrument except the organ.

Challenge Words
autoclave
exclave
subclavian

10. conclave (kŏn′ klāv′, kŏng′ klāv′) [*con = cum* <L. "with"]
n. A private, exclusive, or secret meeting.

To force the College of Cardinals to elect a new pope within a reasonable
time, the doors are locked from both inside and out until the **conclave**
makes a decision.

conclavist, *n.*

11. enclave (ĕn′ klāv′, än′ klāv′) [*en = in* <L. "in"]
n. 1. A country entirely or mostly enclosed within the territory of
another country.

People fleeing persecution often seek refuge inside a foreign embassy,
an **enclave** that is legally part of the country it represents.

2. A district or group isolated or enclosed within a larger one.

Italian merchants trading in Istanbul during the Middle Ages were required to live in an **enclave** beyond the city walls.

enclave, *v.*

Familiar Words
diabetes
diacritic
diagnosis
diagonal
diagram
dialect
dialogue
diameter
diaphanous
diaphragm

DIA <G. "through"

12. diadem (dī ə dĕm) [*dein* <G. "to bind"]
n. A crown or headband worn as a sign of
authority.

Mont Blanc is the monarch of mountains;
    They crowned him long ago
On a throne of rocks, in a robe of clouds,
    With a **diadem** of snow.—Lord Byron

13. diatribe (dī′ ə trīb′) [*tribein* <G. "to rub," "to wear out"]
n. An abusive criticism or attack.

Despite **diatribes** in the press mocking them as "suffragettes," Emmeline
Pankhurst and the Women's Social and Political Union persisted in their
efforts to gain the vote for British women.

<table>
<tr><td>

Challenge Words
dialysis
diapason
diastole
diatom
diatonic

</td></tr>
</table>

14. **diametrical** (dī′ ə mĕt′ rĭ kəl)
[*metron* <G. "measure"]
adj. 1. Pertaining to a diameter.

Prune roses with a **diametrical** cut just above
a leaf bud that grows away from the center of
the bush.

2. Exactly or completely opposite.

The medical profession and the tobacco industry hold **diametrical**
positions on the dangers of cigarette smoking.

diametric, *adj.*

15. **diaspora** (dī ăs′ pər ə) [*speirein* <G. "to scatter"]
n. 1. Any group migration or flight from a
country.

Drought, famine, and civil wars caused a
diaspora throughout the Horn of Africa.

2. (capitalized) The dispersion of the Jews from their homeland in
the Middle East.

The great **Diaspora** occurred in A.D. 70 when Romans captured
Jerusalem, causing thousands of Jews to resettle in cities around the
Mediterranean.

EXERCISE 10A

Circle the letter of the best SYNONYM for the word in bold-faced type.

1. an electronic **clavier**   a. computer   b. keyboard instrument
   c. guitar   d. telephone   e. switchboard
2. the **conclave** of cabinet members   a. grudge   b. forbidden party
   c. secret meeting   d. private opinion   e. hostage
3. despite parental **castigation**   a. chastisement   b. fear   c. delusion
   d. praise   e. adumbrations
4. to avert a(n) **occlusion**   a. accident   b. strike   c. stroke
   d. blockage   e. embarrassing situation
5. the **diadem** of authority   a. pall   b. burden   c. extrusion
   d. scorn   e. crown
6. **diametrically** opposing viewpoints   a. completely   b. slightly
   c. frequently   d. transcendentally   e. creatively
7. an impregnable **enclave**   a. clique   b. minority   c. neighborhood
   d. group surrounded by another   e. group superior to another
8. a(n) **apocryphal** history   a. lucid   b. denigrating   c. authentic
   d. meretricious   e. distorted

9. to deliver a(n) **diatribe**   a. ultimatum   b. anathema   c. message
d. castigating speech   e. valedictory address
10. stricken with **apoplexy**   a. a stroke   b. embarrassment
c. a cataclysm   d. remorse   e. self-consciousness

Circle the letter of the best ANTONYM for the word in bold-faced type.

11. persistent **apostasy**   a. denigration   b. renunciation
c. chastening   d. fidelity   e. prejudice
12. the **reclusive** luminary   a. gregarious   b. appalling   c. egregious
d. world-famous   e. puissant
13. with **chastened** pride   a. undiminished   b. obvious   c. deserving
d. shy   e. infamous

EXERCISE 10B   Circle the letter of the sentence in which the word in bold-faced type is used incorrectly.

1. a. In a tenth-century **diaspora** the Somali people left their traditional homeland in the south of Ethiopa and resettled on the northeast coast of Africa.
   b. Many people regarded the establishment of the state of Israel in 1948 as the end of the **Diaspora** because Jews again took possession of their traditional homeland.
   c. Because many Revolutionary War soldiers accepted payment in frontier acreage, the 1780s saw a **diaspora** of settlers to the rich farmlands of upstate New York and western Pennsylvania.
   d. Defeat in the struggle for independence from Denmark and frustration with poor economic conditions triggered a **diaspora** of Icelanders, who immigrated to Canada and the United States in the 1870s.
2. a. He was so **chastened** by his score of forty percent on the calculus test that his parents felt no need to castigate him further.
   b. **Chastened** by her experience with the big bad wolf, Little Red Riding Hood never again spoke to strangers.
   c. Bathsheba Everdene's calamitous marriage to Sergeant Troy **chastens** her pride and teaches her what qualities to value in a man.
   d. **Chastened** by the opportunity to learn, Yentl disguised herself as a boy and gained admission to the academy.
3. a. If you cut a hailstone **diametrically** and count its layers of ice, you can determine how many times rising currents carried it up to be refrozen before it finally fell to earth.
   b. The position of Margaret Thatcher and her Conservative party was **diametrically** opposed to that of the Labour party on the issue of whether Britain should form closer ties with the European Community.

   c. Although both groups honored traditional Japanese values, **diametrical** political differences separated the leaders of the Meiji Restoration, who wanted imperial power and western-style central government, and their opponents, who favored the shōguns and their sumurai warriors.

   d. Traditional Tibetan women's dress includes a woolen apron woven with bright **diametrical** stripes.

4. a. Wisdom teeth often tend to be **occlusive**, pressing horizontally against the molars rather than vertically through the gums.

   b. The strict **occlusion** of women from New England colleges led Mary Mason Lyon to found Mt. Holyoke, the first American college for women, in 1837.

   c. Dramatic storms often result from an **occluded** front, which occurs when a mass of warm air meets a cold front and is forced to rise over it.

   d. The buildup of cholesterol in blood vessels can lead to their **occlusion**, which may precipitate a heart attack.

5. a. Depictions of Judgment Day as described in the **Apocalypse** were often painted on the rear wall of medieval churches to warn departing churchgoers about what awaited them.

   b. The Aztecs believed that the universe had passed through four previous epochs, each ending in a disaster—famine, fire, hurricane, and flood, respectively—and that the present age would likewise come to **apocalyptic** end.

   c. The creators of the first atomic bomb knew that it could unleash an **apocalypse** of fiery destruction, but they failed to realize the long-range dangers of radiation.

   d. The griffin, an **apocalyptic** animal with the wings of an eagle and the body of a lion, appears frequently on family coats of arms.

6. a. Hungary is a linguistic **enclave**, completely surrounded by unrelated Indo-European languages like Czech, Romanian, Polish, German, and Yugoslavian.

   b. Although located in the heart of Rome, the Vatican is an **enclave** with its own diplomatic corps, militia, and postage stamps.

   c. Helen Thomas, a White House reporter, made an **enclave** into the formerly all-male Gridiron Club.

   d. Following World War II, the Allies divided Berlin, making West Berlin an **enclave** in the midst of the Soviet Zone.

EXERCISE 10C   Fill in each blank with the most appropriate word from Lesson 10. Use a word or any of its forms only once.

1. In order to keep its deliberations strictly secret, the Federal Constitution Convention of 1787 declared itself a(n)

   _____, darkening the windows of Independence Hall and preventing even a scrap of paper from leaving the meeting room.

2. Appearing on a television talk show, Mary McCarthy delivered

   a _____ against her fellow writer Lillian Hellman, claiming her to be "overrated, a bad writer, and a dishonest writer. . . . Every word she writes is a lie, including *and* and *the*."

3. The Byzantine emperor Julian bears the epithet "The

   _____" because he renounced Christianity when he came to the throne and attempted to return the newly converted empire to the worship of Roman gods.

4. Lesotho, one of the bantustans, or self-governing "homelands" established in 1966 exclusively for Africans, is an

   _____ completely surrounded by the Republic of South Africa.

5. Installing hammer action keys into the case of a harpsichord,

   Bartolomeo Cristofori created a new form of _____ that permitted the player to vary the loudness.

6. So many _____ stories have sprung up about the life of the Buddha that historians have difficulty determining which stories are genuine.

7. Although Julian of Norwich once traveled widely on pilgrimages,

   this English mystic became a _____ during her last years, living alone in a tiny cell near her parish church.

8. The Aztec goddess Tlazolteotl, "the Lady of the Witches," is often

   depicted riding a broom and wearing a horned _____ adorned with a crescent moon.

9. "My parents will be _____ when they find out I've wrecked their new car. They're going to kill me!"

10. During the 1980s civil war between the Tamils and the Sinhalese

    peoples of Sri Lanka led to the _____ of more than a million Tamil-speaking people to nearby India.

11. As Tambu adapts to town life after a childhood in the bush, her

    cousin _____ her for being too docile while her uncle seeks to chasten her assertiveness.

EXERCISE 10D   Replace the word or phrase in italics with a key word (or any of its forms) from Lesson 10.

Alfred Nobel (1833–1896) became a wealthy man through his invention and manufacture of dynamite. So acute were his ambitions that nothing served to (1) *discipline* Nobel or curb his drive, not even the deaths of many people, including his brother, when early nitroglycerine experiments exploded. In 1876 he met Bertha Kinsky, a Bohemian noblewoman and one of the world's leading pacifists, who (2) *chastised* him for not taking responsibility for the (3) *enormously destructive* potential of his invention. Although Nobel never became a pacifist, Kinsky inspired him to become a(n) (4) *person who forsakes a principle* and to abandon his previous goal, the unreflecting pursuit of wealth. As a result of this (5) *completely opposite* shift of perspective, Nobel established the Nobel Prizes to promote the welfare of humanity. The Nobel Peace Prize was largely a tribute to Bertha Kinsky.

1. _____   4. _____

2. _____   5. _____

3. _____

REVIEW EXERCISES FOR LESSONS 9 AND 10

1   Circle the letter of the best answer to the following analogies and questions about roots and definitions.

1. remonstrate : praise : :
   a. denigrate : muster
   b. elucidate : confuse
   c. occlude : opened up
   d. adumbrate : castigate
   e. chasten : discipline
2. apostate : faithfulness : :
   a. luminary : darkness
   b. necromancer : black magic
   c. winner : diadem
   d. recluse : gregariousness
   e. elucidator : castigation
3. Which word is not derived from *claudere*?
   a. closet   b. occlude   c. caste   d. close   e. cloister
4. Which name is not derived from *lucere*?
   a. Lucy   b. Lucifer   c. Lucinda   d. Louise   e. Lucille

5. Which root is defined incorrectly?
   a. *apo* <G. "away from"
   b. *monstrare* <L. "monster"
   c. *castus* <L. "pure"
   d. *umbra* <L. "shade"
   e. *dia* <G. "through"

2 Matching: On the line at the left, write the letter of the word or phrase that best describes the newspaper headline or advertisement.

_____ **1.** Candidate for dog catcher labels opponent "soft on spaniels" and a "lab lover."

_____ **2.** Union and management sign agreements after closed session negotiations.

_____ **3.** Counseling from the beyond: get advice from your ancestors. Call Seer's Seance Services today.

_____ **4.** Volunteer firefighters: Meet at firehouse at noon for emergency meeting!

_____ **5.** Principal cites long list of reasons for early retirement.

_____ **6.** Blocked storm drain causes neighborhood flood.

_____ **7.** Accused declared sane and able to stand trial.

A.   conclave

B.   occlusion

C.   necromancy

D.   lucidity

E.   a mustering

F.   elucidation

G.   denigration

3 Fill in each blank with the most appropriate word from Lessons 9 and 10. Use a word or any of its forms only once.

The Industrial Revolution that contributed to the economic success of Victorian England also created the first man-made environmental

a) _____ (widespread destruction). A(n)

b) _____ (dark cover) of black smoke hung permanently over the factory towns of the English Midlands, and as

if by c) _____ (sorcery, black magic), once

d) _____ (crystal clear) rivers ran
black with chemical waste. These factory towns also created
a(n) e) _____ (mass migration) of country
people leaving their villages to find jobs in the cities, where they lived
in cramped, unsanitary conditions.

A similar polluting of the environment and growth of city slums has
occurred in successive nations as they become industrialized, first in
Europe and North America, then in Central and Eastern Europe, and
most recently in Africa and Asia. In response, early environmentalists
f) _____d (severely criticized) industry for
creating these social and natural ills. However, as the complex
relationship between the economy and the natural resources of a
country has become better understood, environmentalists no longer
see their goals as g) _____ly (completely
opposite) different from those of industry, and they have increasingly
moved from launching h) _____s (abusive
attacks) to seeking ways to coordinate the economic and environmental well-being of a region. Likewise, many businesses have begun
to take responsibility for their environmental impact and seek ways to
i) _____ (make less serious) their
reputation as polluters. Though both sides continue to
j) _____ (speak in disapproval) against each
other, they also increasingly acknowledge the necessity of collaboration
for the ultimate good of both the economy and the environment.

4 Writing or Discussion Activities

1. Castigation can occur in many forms, some constructive and others
   hurtful. Imagine a situation in which someone wants to change the
   behavior of a person or group. Write two versions of what the castigator might say, one a diatribe likely to evoke resentment and resistance and the other a gentle chastening likely to create positive results.
2. A teacher whose elucidations are effective can make learning
   easier, while a teacher whose explanations are unclear can cast
   a pall over even a favorite subject. Write a paragraph describing a
   teacher whose lucidity helped you to learn. Try to include concrete
   illustrations and several words from Lessons 9 and 10, especially
   elucidate, lucid, and *pellucid.*
3. Science fiction and ghost stories often appall and delight the
   imagination with descriptions of luminous creatures from another
   world. Using any five words from Lesson 9 and 10, write about an
   encounter with such a nonhuman creature. Include in your writing
   both how the creature looks and how people respond to it.

Military Matters

LESSON 11

Paritur pax bello.
Peace is begotten of war.—CORNELIUS NEPOS

Key Words		
abate	carte blanche	fortitude
battery	cartel	impugn
battlement	cartographer	indomitable
bellicose	daunt	pugilist
belligerent	forte	pugnacious

Familiar Words
bat
batter
battle
combat
combatant
debate
noncombatant
rebate

BATTUO, BATTUERE, BATTUI, BATTUUM <L. "to beat," "to knock"

1. **battery** (băt′ ə rē)
   n. 1. A beating or pounding, especially an unlawful beating, as in assault and battery.

   "Running the gauntlet" was once a legal form of **battery** in which the offender had to run between two rows of men who beat him with weapons as he passed.

   2. Guns or heavy artillery.

   In a disastrous charge immortalized by Alfred, Lord Tennyson, in "The Charge of the Light Brigade," British cavalry armed only with swords attacked Russian cannon emplacements:
   Plunged in the **battery**-smoke
   Right thro' the line they broke. . . .

103

3. A group of similar things used together.

The Stanford-Binet Intelligence Scale seeks to determine a person's so-called Intelligence Quotient (I.Q.) by a **battery** of tests including recognition of categories, analogies, antonyms, and absurdities.

NOTA BENE: Used to mean "a group of similar things used together" *battery* has several specialized meanings: the pitcher and catcher on a baseball team, the percussion section of an orchestra, and a device for generating electric current. The legal term *assault and battery* has two specific parts: *assault* refers to a threat to use force on someone, while *battery* refers to an actual carrying out of that threat.

2. **battlement**   (băt′ əl mənt)
   n. A defense wall with alternating high and low sections (often used in plural form).

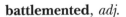

In the opening scene of *Hamlet*, guards encounter the ghost of the former king walking on the **battlements** of Elsinore Castle.

battlemented, *adj.*

3. **abate**   (ə bāt′)   [*a* = *ad* <L. "to," "toward"]
   intr. v. To reduce in quantity or intensity; to subside; to diminish.

When a sudden storm interrupts their hunt, Aeneas and Dido take shelter in a cave until the rain **abates**.

abatement, *n.*

BELLUM <L. "war"

4. **bellicose**   (bĕl ĭ kōs′)
   adj. Warlike; eager to fight.

"All successful newspapers are ceaselessly querulous and **bellicose**."
—Henry L. Mencken

bellicoseness, *n.*; **bellicosity**, *n.*

5. **belligerent**   (bə lĭj′ ər ənt)
   [*genere* <L. "to bear"]
   n. A country or persons engaged in warfare or hostile action.

Before Roman gladiators fought, both **belligerents** greeted the emperor with the Latin phrase *Morituri te salutamus*, "We who are about to die salute you."

adj. Behaving in a hostile or aggressive manner; engaged in combat.

Hoping to achieve "peace for our time," Britain's prime minister Neville Chamberlain signed the 1938 Munich Pact condoning Germany's **belligerent** policy of *lebensraum*, seizing "living space" from other countries.

belligerence, *n.*; **belligerency**, *n.*

<table>
<tr><td>**Familiar Word**
undaunted</td></tr>
</table>

DOMO, DOMARE, DOMUI, DOMITUM <L. "to tame," "to subdue"

6. **daunt**   (dŏnt, dănt)
   tr. v. To intimidate; to discourage or dishearten.

   Wilma Rudolph refused to let the inability to walk until the age of eight **daunt** her; she went on to win three Olympic gold medals in track and field.

   daunting, *adj.*; **dauntless**, *adj.*

7. **indomitable**   (ĭn dŏm' ə tə bəl)   [*in* <L. "not"]
   adj. Unconquerable.

   The **indomitable** armies of Queen Amina made Zaria the most powerful of the Hausa States of West Africa.

   indomitability, *n.*; **indomitableness**, *n.*

<table>
<tr><td>**Familiar Words**
comfort
effort
enforce
fortify
fortress
reinforce</td></tr>
</table>

FORTIS <L. "strong"

8. **forte**   (fôrt, fōrt)
   n. A person's strong point; the thing in which a person excels.

   Although she has played serious dramatic roles, Whoopi Goldberg's **forte** is comedy.

   adj. (fōr' tā´) In music, loudly; forcefully.

   The notation *f* in a piece of music indicates where a composer wishes a passage to be played **forte**; the notation *p* indicates piano, or "softly."

9. **fortitude**   (fōr' tə tōod, fōr' tə tyōod)
   n. Courage in enduring pain or trouble.

   Flora Macdonald became a Scottish hero for her **fortitude** in the rescue of Bonnie Prince Charlie, smuggling him to safety disguised as her maid.

   fortitudinous, *adj.*

<table>
<tr><td>**Challenge Words**
deforce
fortis
fortissimo
pianoforte</td></tr>
</table>

KHARTES <G. "leaf of papyrus," "a writing"

10. **carte blanche**   (kärt blänsh'; plural **cartes blanches**: kärt blänsch', kärt blän' shĭz)   [*blanche* <Fr. "white" <L. *blancus*, "white"]
    n. Unrestricted power to act at one's discretion; unconditional permission or authority.

    According to the principles of laissez-faire economics, companies should have **carte blanche** to conduct business without government interference.

11. **cartel**   (kär tĕl')
    n. 1. An organization of firms in the same industry for the purpose of regulating production, pricing, and marketing of goods and decreasing competition by members.

    Developing countries that produce oil formed the Organization of Petroleum Exporting Countries (OPEC), a **cartel** that seeks to control oil production rates.

    2. A coalition of political or special-interest groups to achieve a common cause; a bloc.

    Because the rivers where Northwest salmon spawn have become polluted, Native Americans and environmentalists have formed a **cartel** to protect the fish from extinction.

    cartelist, *n.*; **cartelization**, *n.*; **cartelize**, *v.*

12. **cartographer**   (kär tŏg' rə fər)   [*graphein* <G. "to write"]
    n. A maker of maps or charts.

    The Swiss, the world's most outstanding **cartographers** of mountain ranges, have constructed a detailed map of Mt. Everest using aerial photographs.

    cartographic, *adj.*; **cartographical**, *adj.*; **cartography**, *n.*

PUGNO, PUGNARE, PUGNAVI, PUGNATUM <L. "to fight"

13. **pugilist**   (pyōō' jə lĭst)
    n. A fistfighter, especially a professional boxer.

    The Gemini, Castor and Pollux, were famed for their accomplishments, Castor as a horse trainer and Pollux as a **pugilist**.

    pugilism, *n.*; **pugilistic**, *adj.*

14. **pugnacious** (pŭg nā′ shəs)
    adj. Quarrelsome; eager for a fight.

    "It is unfair to blame man too fiercely for being **pugnacious**; he has learned it from Nature."—Christopher Morley

    pugnacity, *n.*

15. **impugn** (ĭm pyo͞on′) [*im* = *in* <L. "not"]
    tr. v. To oppose or attack as false; to seek to discredit.

    Although Queen Elizabeth I **impugned** her cousin Mary, Queen of Scots, as a "wicked murderess" who had plotted her assassination, Mary's execution caused the queen great grief.

    impugnable, *adj.*; **impugnability**, *n.*; **impugner**, *n.*

NOTA BENE: Both *pugnacious* and *bellicose* mean "eager to fight," but the two words differ in usage. *Pugnacious* usually describes an individual, someone who is bad tempered or who enjoys picking a fight. *Bellicose* more often describes a nation or an institution, such as a government with an aggressive military policy of conquest.

Belligerent can apply to both aggressive persons and groups but differs from *pugnacious* and *bellicose* in also describing a state of actual engagement in warfare; for example, The belligerent forces made a truce.

EXERCISE 11A

Circle the letter of the best SYNONYM for the word(s) in bold-faced type.

1. a contest of **pugilism**   a. warfare   b. wills   c. endurance
   d. fencing   e. boxing
2. to show a(n) **fortitudinous** spirit   a. generous   b. courageous
   c. stubborn   d. politic   e. aggressive
3. to fear **impugners**   a. belligerents   b. creditors   c. discreditors
   d. interlopers   e. demagogues
4. to give them **cartes blanches**   a. white maps   b. blank charts
   c. full power   d. honorary degrees   e. clean slates
5. an improvement in **cartography**   a. legerdemain   b. card tricks
   c. transportation   d. mapmaking   e. record keeping
6. to reinforce the **battlements**   a. argument   b. troops
   c. defensive walls   d. belligerents   e. ill will

7. **daunted** by the challenge   a. disarmed   b. deterred
   c. subsidized   d. sublimated   e. unintimidated
8. recognized his **forte**   a. strong point   b. courage   c. talent
   d. acumen   e. defensive walls
9. a(n) **indomitable** potentate   a. famous   b. bellicose   c. altruistic
   d. unconquerable   e. dubious

Circle the letter of the best ANTONYM for the word in bold-faced type.

10. an empire known for **bellicosity**   a. pacifism   b. beauty
    c. pugnacity   d. acquisitiveness   e. altercations
11. the **abatement** of the crowd   a. growth   b. transcendence
    c. pugnacity   d. enthusiasm   e. encouragement
12. demonstrated **pugnacity**   a. boxing   b. reluctance to fight
    c. belligerence   d. egregiousness   e. suspicion of strangers

EXERCISE 11B   Circle the letter of the sentence in which the word in bold-faced type is used incorrectly.

1. a. The Quota Act of 1921, legislation to restrict immigration, was promoted by a **cartel** of "nativists," who feared new immigrants not of a northern European Protestant background.
   b. French aristocrats rode to their execution by guillotine in a tumbrel, a small peasant **cartel**.
   c. Medieval guilds functioned like **cartels**, setting standards and prices for their products.
   d. Kemal Atatürk came to power with the support of the Young Turks, a **cartel** that supported his reformist policies.
2. a. Before the **belligerents** in the Vietnam War would sit down at the negotiating table, they debated for weeks over the shape of that table.
   b. Reminded of the women warriors of Greek mythology, European explorers named the Amazon River after the **belligerent** native women they met along its banks.
   c. According to the Geneva Convention, a set of international rules of conduct during warfare, all hospitals are officially neutral and not to be treated **belligerently**.
   d. As an inducement, all **belligerents** who finish the race will receive T-shirts.
3. a. The fortepiano, a precursor of the modern piano, received this name because it could play piano, or softly, as well as **forte**.
   b. Though sports were never my **forte**, I have become an accomplished skateboard artist.
   c. After retiring as a singer, Beverly Sills developed another **forte** as the general director of the New York City Opera.

      d. The Assyrian army of King Sennacherib appeared **forte** and indomitable at sunset, but at sunrise lay dead, overcome by a mysterious plague spread by "the Angel of Death."

4. a. Pugilists wear padded gloves to reduce their **battery** power.

      b. Astronauts returning from space must undergo a **battery** of tests to measure the effects of weightlessness.

      c. To perform Tchaikovsky's *1812* Overture, which imitates the sounds of cannons and church bells, the **battery** of a symphony orchestra must be enlarged.

      d. Despite the fire from German **batteries**, Allied troops managed to establish beachheads on the coast of Normandy.

EXERCISE 11C   Fill in each blank with the most appropriate word from Lesson 11. Use a word or any of its forms only once.

1. The nation's shock at the murder of Martin Luther King, Jr., had

not _____ when Senator Robert F. Kennedy was assassinated two months later.

2. _____ often suffer "cauliflower ears," a disfigurement in which the cartilage of the ears becomes malformed from frequent battering.

3. Although she was criticized and demoted, Anna Julia Cooper's

_____ efforts to promote educational excellence for African-Americans resulted in many students gaining admission to Ivy League colleges.

4. Obviously losing, the debaters resorted to *argumentation ad hominem,*

attempting to _____ their opponents' characters rather than attacking their ideas.

5. For more than forty years a _____ of scholars monopolized the Dead Sea Scrolls, preventing others from studying the valuable biblical manuscripts.

6. The legendary thirteenth-century Vietnamese warrior sisters Trung-Nhi and Trung-Trac defended their territory for a decade

with great _____ against powerful Chinese invaders.

7. The threat of death did not _____ Antigone's pious determination to bury her dishonored brother.

8. Basing their information on the oral reports of explorers,

early _____ represented California as an island lying northwest of Mexico.

9. Take my credit card; I give you _____
   to purchase what we need for the trip.

10. Left undefended when the Roman army retreated from
    Britain, the agrarian Celts were easily conquered by the

    _____ Germanic tribes of Angles,
    Saxons, and Jutes.

11. As Sir Gawain approached the castle of the Green Knight,

    he noticed its strong towers and _____
    silhouetted against the winter sky "as if cut out of paper."

12. Both gods and mortals were _____ in the
    Trojan War, Hera and Poseidon championing the Greeks and
    Venus supporting the Trojans.

EXERCISE 11D   Replace the word or phrase in italics with a key word (or any of its forms)
from Lesson 11.

All Quiet on the Western Front recounts the (1) *unsurmountable* (2)
courage in enduring pain of common soldiers in the trenches of World
War I. (3) *Discouraged* by miserable conditions and hours of assaults
by enemy (4) *heavy artillery*, these ordinary (5) *combatants* find comfort
only in their friendships with each other. They (6) *oppose as false* their
(7) *warlike* national policies, their arrogant officers, and even their families, who continue to regard war as glorious and heroic. The author,
Erich Maria Remarque, died in the war, but the power of his antiwar
theme has continued without (8) *diminishment* since its publication in
the 1920s.

1. _____   5. _____

2. _____   6. _____

3. _____   7. _____

4. _____   8. _____

LESSON 12

Multa cedicerunt ut altius surgerent.
Many things have fallen only to rise again.—SENECA

Key Words

accede	concession	Occident
cadence	decadent	predatory
casuistry	depredation	punctilious
cede	expunge	pungent
compunction	intercede	recidivism

Familiar Words
accident
cadaver
cascade
case
casual
chance
cheat
chute
coincide
decay
deciduous
incident
occasion
parachute

Challenge Words
cadent
cadenza
caducous
casus belli
escheat

CADO, CADERE, CECIDI, CASUM <L. "to fall," "to come to an end"

1. **cadence**   (kād′ əns)
   n. A rhythmic flow of sound, as in poetry or oratory, or of movement, as in marching or dancing.

   Good ideas, asserts John Dryden, make an impact even when badly expressed: "Wit will shine / Through the harsh **cadence** of a rugged line."

2. **casuistry**   (kăzh′ o͞o ĭ strē)
   n. 1. The use of moral principles to reason out what is right or wrong in everyday situations (usually associated with a morality that emphasizes adherence to established laws).

   Chinese scholars of Confucius use **casuistry** to determine from ancient texts how contemporary moral problems should be solved.

   2. Subtle but misleading or false application of reasoning; a quibbling or evasive way of making difficult decisions.

   Alexander Pope attacked false logic as the enemy of truth: "See skulking Truth to her old cavern fled, / Mountains of **casuistry** heap'd o'er her head!"

   casuist, *n.*; **casuistic**, *adj.*; **casuistical**, *adj.*

3. **decadent**   (dĕk′ ə dənt, dĭ kād′ ənt)   [*de* <L. "away from"]
   adj. Declining or decaying (applied to a condition, things, or people).

   In the centuries that followed the reign of Suleiman the Magnificent, the Ottoman Empire became increasingly **decadent**, its territory shrinking and its internal structure eroding to the point that nineteenth-century politicians referred to it as "the sick man of Europe."

n. 1. A person who is decaying mentally or morally.

After the Russian Revolution middle-class writers like Anna Akhmatova were condemned as **decadents** because they wrote subjective lyrics rather than praise of the new socialist state.

2. (usually capitalized) A member of a group of nineteenth-century French and English artists who were inspired by artificial and morbid things.

The operetta *Patience* mocks the "art for art's sake" credo of the **Decadents**, as embodied in the foppish Bunthorne:
> A pallid and thin young man,
> A haggard and lank young man,
> A greenery yallery, Grosvenor Gallery,
> Foot-in-the-grave young man!

decadence, *n.*

4. **Occident**   (ŏk′ sĭ dənt, ŏk′ sĭ dĕnt)
n. (capitalized) The parts of the world that lie west of Asia, especially the countries of Europe and the western hemisphere.

Although Islamic merchants had long traded with Asia, Chinese technological achievements such as gunpowder, paper, and silk reached the **Occident** only after the Crusades.

Occidental, occidental, *adj.*; **Occidentalism**, *n.*; **occidentalize**, *v.*

5. **recidivism**   (rĕ sĭd′ ə vĭz′ əm)   [*re* <L. "back," "again"]
n. A relapse into a former habit, especially criminal or antisocial behavior.

Counseling and job training can cut **recidivism** among juvenile offenders to twenty-five percent, compared with fifty percent among youths without such support.

recidivist, *n.*; **recidivistic**, *adj.*; **recidivous**, *adj.*

CEDO, CEDERE, CESSI, CESSUM <L. "to move," "to yield"

6. **cede**   (sēd)
tr. v. To yield or surrender rights or possessions, usually officially.

In the 1803 Louisiana Purchase, France **ceded** to the United States the land extending from the Mississippi River to the Rocky Mountains in return for fifteen million dollars.

7. **accede**   (ăk sēd′)   [*ac* = *ad* <L. "to," "toward"]
intr. v. To consent; to agree (used with *to*).

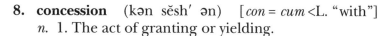

Familiar Words
abscess
access
ancestor
antecedent
cease
decease
exceed
necessary
precede
precedent
predecessor
proceed
recede
recess
recession
secede
success

Challenge Words
cession
concessive
retrocede

Catherine Sloper refuses to **accede** to her father's demand that she break her engagement to Morris Townsend, a penniless fortune hunter.

2. To take office; to become a ruler (used with *to*).

When she **acceded** to her father's position and lands, Eleanor of Aquitaine became one of the most powerful rulers in Europe.

accession, *n.*; **accessional**, *adj.*

8. **concession**   (kən sĕsh′ ən)   [*con* = *cum* <L. "with"]
n. 1. The act of granting or yielding.

In an eighteenth-century version of "No pain, no gain," Fanny Burney observed, "[W]here **concession** is made without pain, it is often made without meaning."

2. Permission by authority for special use, especially the privilege of setting up a business in a certain place, or the place itself.

To help the seniors raise money for their class trip, the administration has granted them an exclusive **concession** to sell refreshments during basketball games.

concede, *v.*; **concessionaire**, *n.*; **concessionary**, *adj.*

NOTA BENE: *Cede* and *concede* both have the same meaning: "to surrender rights." However, *concede* has the additional meaning "to admit" or "to make a concession." For example, I concede that I was impolite, but I certainly wasn't pugnacious.

9. **intercede**   (ĭn tər sēd′)
[*inter* <L. "between"]
intr. v. 1. To act on another's behalf.

Cupid, who wishes to marry the mortal Psyche, **intercedes** with Jupiter, asking that Psyche be permitted to eat ambrosia and thus become immortal.

2. To mediate in a dispute; to seek to reconcile differences.

When the management of a business and the workers' union cannot resolve a dispute, a judge often appoints a mediator to **intercede**.

intercession, *n.*; **intercessor**, *n.*

PRAEDA <L. "spoils of war," "plunder," "booty"

10. **predatory**   (prĕd´ ə tôr´ ē, prĕd´ ə tōr´ ē)
    [*pre* <L. "before"]
    adj. 1. Preying on other animals.

    Predatory birds like hawks or eagles are
    distinguished by their sharp beaks, which
    are adapted for tearing flesh.

    2. Plundering; exploiting or victimizing others.

    "The sun and the moon and the stars would have disappeared long
    ago . . .; had they happened to be within the reach of **predatory**
    human hands."—Havelock Ellis

    predation, *n.*; **predator**, *n.*; **predatoriness**, *n.*

11. **depredation**   (dĕp´ rə dā´ shən)   [*de* <L. "away from"]
    n. Destruction; plunder.

    When their territory becomes overgrazed, elephants can cause wide-
    spread environmental **depredation** by uprooting trees and shrubbery.

    depredate, *v.*; **depredator**, *n.*; **depredatory**, *adj.*

PUNGO, PUNGERE, PUPUGI, PUNCTUM
<L. "to prick," "to puncture"

12. **punctilious**   (pŭngk tĭl´ ē əs)
    adj. Precise; scrupulous; attentive to
    details, especially of etiquette.

    For success at the court of Louis XIV,
    Madame de Maintenon advised **punctilious**
    decorum.

    punctiliousness, *n.*

13. **pungent**   (pən´ jənt)
    adj. Having a strong, biting taste or smell.

    Jude Fawley realizes from the **pungent** odor of
    incense in her clothes that Sue Bridehead has
    begun to attend church.

    pungency, *n.*

14. **compunction**   (kəm pəngk´ shən)   [*con* = *cum* <L. "with"]
    n. Uneasiness caused by guilt; remorse; scruples.

"The beginning of **compunction** is the beginning of a new life."
—George Eliot

compunctious, *adj.*

15. **expunge** (ĕk spŭnj′, ĭk spŭnj′) [*ex* <L. "from," "out of"]
tr. v. To omit; to delete; to obliterate.

The court will **expunge** this speeding ticket from your record if you attend traffic school.

expunction, *n.*; **expunger**, *n.*

EXERCISE 12A   Circle the letter of the best SYNONYM for the word(s) in bold-faced type.

1. exhibit **decadence**   a. spirit   b. moral decay   c. acrimony
   d. talent   e. legerdemain
2. accused of being a(n) **recidivist**   a. person incapable of reform
   b. liar   c. dreamer   d. alcoholic   e. person incapable of being
   on time
3. **expunction of** her name   a. explanation of   b. pronuciation of
   c. confusion over   d. traduction of   e. removal of
4. to need a(n) **intercessor**   a. mediator   b. interim   c. assistant
   d. teacher   e. translator
5. the **pungency** of her wit   a. subtlety   b. acrimony   c. originality
   d. daring   e. sharpness
6. to **cede** the microphone   a. seize   b. refuse to allow   c. give up
   d. wire   e. permit
7. the rapid **cadence**   a. rhythm   b. sound   c. dance   d. parameter
   e. chatter
8. a notorious **casuist**   a. person who intercedes   b. recluse
   c. demagogue   d. necromancer   e. person who uses false
   reasoning
9. to expect **punctiliousness**   a. tardiness   b. meticulousness
   c. sloppiness   d. belligerence   e. the best
10. a(n) **compunctious** attitude   a. resentful   b. exploitative
    c. annoying   d. altruistic   e. contrite
11. to undergo **depredation**   a. destruction   b. denigration
    c. apostasy   d. altercation   e. suffering

Circle the letter of the best ANTONYM for the word in bold-faced type.

12. to announce his **accession**   a. victory   b. demise   c. intentions
    d. resignation   e. rejection
13. to **concede** the election   a. challenge   b. exult at   c. accept
    d. regret   e. surrender
14. to originate in the **Occident**   a. west   b. past   c. east
    d. archipelago   e. mind

EXERCISE 12B   Circle the letter of the sentence in which the word in bold-faced type is
                     used incorrectly.

1. a. With almost no **predators** to inhibit their reproduction, kangaroo
       populations frequently outpace available food.
    b. In search of a wealthy husband, Becky Sharp attends social
       functions with a **predatory** fervor.
    c. **Predatory** mine owners paid their employees in scrip that could
       be redeemed only at the company-owned store, which charged
       exorbitant prices.
    d. Running for class office in our school is **predatory** on
       maintaining a 2.0 grade point average.

2. a. To protect themselves from thunderstorms and fire, medieval
       people often prayed for the **intercession** of Saint Barbara, who
       later became the patron saint of firefighters.
    b. In recognition of her tireless **intercession** with the government
       on behalf of the indigenous peoples of Guatemala, Rigoberta
       Menchu was awarded the Nobel Peace Prize.
    c. The sly Brer Rabbit **intercedes** with Brer Fox not to throw him in
       the briarpatch, which is, in fact, his home territory.
    d. With the help of an **intercessor**, the bitter child custody dispute
       was resolved.

3. a. Aubrey Beardsley's grisly illustrations of Edgar Allan Poe's story
       "The Masque of the Red Death" epitomize the macabre taste of
       the **Decadents**.
    b. Le Corbusier frequently designed **decadent** ramps to connect
       the entrances of his buildings with the surrounding landscape.
    c. Some nineteenth-century historians attributed the fall of the
       Roman Empire to a moral and physical **decadence** resulting from
       taking too many baths.
    d. Although Dorian Gray leads the life of a **decadent**, his good looks
       never fade; his portrait, however, changes to reflect his growing
       moral corruption.

4. a. Special parking spaces close to entrances provide people with
       disabilities easier **accession** to public buildings.
    b. The U.S. Constitution provides that if the president dies or is
       incapacitated for any reason, the vice-president shall **accede** to
       the presidency.
    c. While visiting Kenya in 1952 Elizabeth learned of her **accession**
       to the throne.
    d. Think for yourself! Don't **accede** to everything the group suggests.

5. a. The United States Department of the Interior sells **concessions**
       to private lumber companies to cut timber on government lands.
    b. During the holidays, many stores permit **concessionaires**, often
       dressed as Santa Claus and ringing bells, to raise money for
       charity outside their entrances.

    c. Because it had to be imported from the Baltic, salt was a very expensive **concession** in medieval Europe and was thus used sparingly.

    d. Urging countries to **concede** national interests to achieve international peace, Eleanor Roosevelt asserted that "cooperation may imply compromise, but if it brings a world advance it is a gain for each individual nation."

EXERCISE 12C   Fill in each blank with the most appropriate word from Lesson 12. Use a word or any of its forms only once.

1. In *The Odyssey* the entrance to the underworld lies in the

   _____, a region associated with death because the sun "dies" there daily.

2. African drumming is polyrhythmic, with the master drummer

   setting the _____, on which each additional drummer makes complementary variations.

3. Drug rehabilitation programs have a very high rate of

   _____ if the former addicts return directly to the same environment and circumstances where they originally became addicted.

4. Cooks prize cilantro for the _____ bite this herb adds to soups, sauces, and salads.

5. Although they appear to be harmless plants, sea anemones are

   actually _____ animals, which stun and devour fish that swim into their "petals."

6. Proper performance of the traditional Japanese tea ceremony,

   which requires _____ execution of every gesture, takes years of training.

7. The _____ of Catch-22 deeply impresses Yossarian: "[A pilot] would be crazy to fly more missions and sane if he didn't; but if he was sane he had to fly them. If he flew them he was crazy and didn't have to, but if he didn't want to he was sane and had to."

8. Winston Smith's job in the Ministry of Truth is to

   _____ from all records the mention of events that the government declares "never happened."

9. Because it was spared the bombing raids that caused widespread

   _____ elsewhere, Prague is the best-preserved baroque city in Europe.

10. The agnostic Charles Ryder struggles to understand the

_____ that prevents Julia, a divorced Roman
Catholic, from marrying him.

11. Unable to maintain their ancient Welsh castle, the family agreed

to _____ it to The National Trust, which
would make the much-needed repairs and open it to the public.

EXERCISE 12D   Replace the word or phrase in italics with a key word (or any of its forms)
from Lesson 12.

   During the Cultural Revolution in China the Red Guards sought to
(1) *eradicate totally* what they perceived as threats to the revolution. They
branded many intellectuals as (2) *morally corrupt persons* and chastised
them with public humiliations. Even party members who had become
well-off were accused of (3) *lapsing into old habits* associated with capi-
talism and influences from the (4) *countries west of Asia*. Because the Red
Guards had the support of Chairman Mao, few people dared (5) *to
act on behalf of* those being persecuted, and even government officials
who privately disapproved of their actions nevertheless (6) *gave consent*
to their demands.

1. _____   4. _____

2. _____   5. _____ for

3. _____   6. _____

REVIEW EXERCISES FOR LESSONS 11 AND 12

1   Circle the letter of the best answer to the following analogies and
questions about roots and definitions.

1. decadence : decaying : :
   a. concession : interceding
   b. expunction : sponging
   c. belligerence : dominating
   d. forte : fighting
   e. intimidation : daunting
2. pugilist : fistfight : :
   a. cartographer : map
   b. casuist : logic
   c. belligerent : warfare

      d. intercessor : concession

      e. impugner : defense

3. Which word does not have a "point," i.e., does not derive from *pungere?*   a. compunction   b. punctual   c. punctilious   d. impugn   e. disappoint

4. Which word does not derive from *cadere?*

      a. cadence b. casuistry c. accede d. decadent e. Occident

5. Which root is defined incorrectly?

      a. *domare* <L. "to subdue"   d. *cadere* <L. "to fall"

      b. *pungere* <L. "to point"   e. *praeda* <L. "spoils of war"

      c. *cedere* <L. "to yield"

2   Eavesdropping in the Cafeteria

Matching: On the line at the left, write the letter of the noun that best matches the quotation.

A. recidivism   D. concession   F. punctiliousness

B. cartel   E. casuistry   G. abatement

C. intercession   H. compunction

_____ **1.** "I know you're angry, but he's really hurt. Each of you should try to understand how the other feels."

_____ **2.** "They can't convert our practice field to a parking lot! Let's get the baseball, soccer, and hockey teams to demonstrate with us."

_____ **3.** "Well, I really loved this book when I started it, but it gradually got less and less interesting until finally I just couldn't finish it."

_____ **4.** "When we left the prom at 11:37, I shook hands with all the chaperons and thanked each one. Then I had my date home by 11:59."

_____ **5.** "My curfew is midnight, and I really was home by then because my foot was across the threshold. But then I stood there talking at the door for two hours, and now my parents say I came in late. But I was already in, wasn't I?"

_____ **6.** "Yes, I know I got busted for cheating before. And I know I haven't done it for a whole year, but, hey, this time I've got a really foolproof method."

_____ **7.** "I asked Diego to the party when I thought he had broken up with Dona. Then they got back together, so I asked Dave. Then Diego and Dona broke up again. Now Dona blames me for their split, I've got two dates, and I feel awful."

_____ **8.** "All right, just pay me back $20 of the $25 you owe me. But let me borrow your car sometime, okay?"

3   Fill in each blank with the most appropriate word from Lessons 11 and 12. Use a word or any of its forms only once.

In the *Art of Poetry*, Aristotle describes the ideal tragic hero as someone "whose misfortune comes about not because of vice or

a) _____ (moral decay) but through some error of judgment." Aristotle cites Oedipus in Sophocles' tragedy *King Oedipus* as an example because although the hero was able to

b) _____ (intimidate) the

c) _____ (plundering) Sphinx and

d) _____ (to become ruler) to the throne of

Thebes, he was not e) _____ (unconquerable) because he did not know who he really was.

Oedipus believed himself to be the son of the king and queen of Corinth. However, when many years earlier he received a prophecy that he would kill his father and marry his mother, he had fled Corinth to evade that possibility. Thus when the prophet Teiresias

f) _____ (seeks to discredit) him as a parricide,

Oedipus responds g) _____ ly (aggressively).

Confident of his identity, he makes no h) _____s (compromises) to his wife Jocasta's pleas to stop trying to learn the

truth. His confidence begins to i) _____ (diminish), however, when he learns that he is an adopted child. In the end Oedipus discovers the truth that in seeking to flee the prophecy, he has only fulfilled it, but even as he recognizes his error of judgment, he retains his heroic status, accepting his fate with noble

j) _____ (courage in enduring trouble).

4   Writing or Discussion Activities

1. Describe one of your fortes. How did you come to recognize it? How have you developed or used it? Do you wish to develop or use it further?
2. Write a dialogue between two people each of whom illustrates a quality or attitude listed below. Do not use the two descriptive words in your dialogue but let these qualities or attitudes show in what the people say to each other. Read your dialogue to your classmates to see if they can guess which two attitudes your characters illustrate.

pugnacity	punctiliousness	umbrage	compunction
fortitude	predatoriness	decadence	intercession

3. The word *battery* has many meanings, as the definitions and Nota Bene information indicate. Make up four sentences that illustrate different ways that *battery* can be used.

Good and Bad

LESSON 13

Nostra sine auxilio fugiunt bona; carpite florem.
Our good things fly away without our control: pluck the flower.—OVID

Key Words

aesthete	benignant	boon
aesthetic	benison	debonair
beatific	bona fide	eugenics
beatitude	bonanza	euphemism
benign	bon vivant	euphony

Familiar Word
anesthesia

AISTHANESTHAI <G. "to perceive"

1. **aesthete** (ĕs' thēt)
   n. A person who cultivates a superior appreciation of beauty, especially in the arts; often used to imply that the person's appreciation is excessive, affected, or impractical.

   William Morris's advice to the aspiring **aesthete** was to "Have nothing in your house that you do not know to be useful, or believe to be beautiful."

2. **aesthetic**   (ĕs´ thĕ´ tĭk)
adj. Pertaining to an appreciation of beauty.

"Art is the imposing of a pattern on experience, and our **aesthetic** enjoyment in recognition of the pattern."—Alfred North Whitehead

aesthetical, *adj.*; **aesthetician**, *n.*; **aestheticism**, *n.*; **aesthetics**, *n.*

NOTA BENE: *Aesthete* and *aesthetic* can also be correctly spelled *esthete* and *esthetic*, and their related words can be spelled with an *ae* or an *e*. The error is to mix spellings, both of which represent attempts to reproduce in English the first sound of the Greek root *aisthanesthai*.

BEO, BEARE, BEAVI, BEATUM <L. "to make blessed"

Familiar Word Beatrice

3. **beatific**   (bē ə tĭf´ ĭk)   [*facere* <L. "to make," "to do"]
adj. Demonstrating extreme joy or blessedness.

Although their personal relationship was belligerent, on stage the actors managed to appear as **beatific** newlyweds.

beatify, *v.*

Challenge Word beautify

4. **beatitude**   (bē ăt´ ə tōōd´, bē ăt´ ə tyōōd´)
n. 1. Supreme blessedness; exalted happiness.

In the Buddhist tradition a person who has achieved a state of **beatitude** is termed a *bodhisattva*.

2. (capitalized with *the*) A series of declarations about blessedness made by Jesus in the Sermon on the Mount.

"Blessed are the peacemakers" is one of the **Beatitudes**.

BENE <L. "well"

Familiar Words Benedict benediction benefactor beneficial benefit benevolence nota bene (N.B.)

5. **benign**   (bĭ nīn´)
adj. 1. Kindly; mild and gentle in effect.

When from our better selves we have too long
Been parted by the hurrying world,. . .
How gracious, how **benign**, is Solitude.—William Wordsworth

2. Not malignant, as a growth or tumor.

To determine whether a tumor is malignant or **benign**, doctors perform a biopsy, an examination of the cellular structure of a small piece of tumor tissue.

benignity, *n.*

6. **benignant**   (bĭ nĭg′ nənt)
   adj. Beneficial; kindly.

   For her **benignant** work among Italian immigrants, Mother Francesca Cabrini became the first American saint in the Catholic church.

   Antonym: **malignant**

7. **benison**   (bĕn′ ə zən, bĕn′ ə sən)
   n. A blessing or benediction.

   In "The Great Lover," Rupert Brooke lists among the things he most loves "the **benison** of hot water."

BONUS <L. "good"

8. **bona fide**   (bō′ nə fīd, bŏ′ nə fī′ dē)   [*fide* <L. *fides*, "trust," "faith"]
   adj. Authentic; genuine.

   The museum identified the straw jar as a **bona fide** Apache *olla*, decorated with geometric forms and lined with pine pitch to make it watertight.

9. **bonanza**   (bə năn′ zə)
   n. 1. A rich mass of ore.

   In 1859 J.H. Gregory discovered a rich vein of gold in Colorado, a **bonanza** that led to the Pike's Peak gold rush.

   2. An unexpected source of great wealth or luck; a windfall.

   The discovery of uranium on reservation lands has been a **bonanza** for the Navajo nation.

10. **bon vivant**   (bôn vē vän′, bôn vē vänt′;
    plural **bons vivants**: bôn vē vän′, bôn vē vänts′)
    [*vivant* <French "alive" <L. *vivere*, "to live"]
    n. A person who enjoys good food and drink and lives luxuriously.

    During the Great Depression of the 1930s the American public preferred films about the fabulous lives of **bons vivants** and millionaires to realistic dramas about contemporary problems.

11. **boon**   (bo͞on)
    adj. Jolly; convivial (usually used with *companion*).

    Before his accession to the throne as King Henry V, young Prince Hal enjoys escapades with his **boon** companion Falstaff.

n. A benefit greatly enjoyed.

Floods and fires that are destructive to human life often prove to be a **boon** to wildlife by renewing their habitats.

NOTA BENE: The archaic use of *boon*, which often occurs in fairy tales and legends, means "a blessing" or "a request or favor greatly desired." For example, when young Sir Percival comes to Camelot naive and untrained, he begs a boon of King Arthur to be allowed to fight a knight who has just insulted Queen Guinevere.

12. **debonair**   (dĕb ə nâr´)   [*de* <L. "away from"]
    adj. Suave; urbane; nonchalant.

    Jay Gatsby's attempts to impress Daisy with his wealth and his **debonair** manners turn out to be futile.

EU <G. "good"

13. **eugenics**   (yōō jĕn´ ĭks)   [*gen* <G. *genos, geneos,* "race," "family"]
    n. (plural in form but used with a singular verb) The study of improving a species, especially human beings, by genetic control such as discouraging the reproduction of individuals presumed to have undesirable innate traits and encouraging the reproduction of those with desirable traits.

    Through **eugenics** cattle breeders have produced the beefalo, a cross between the buffalo and the cow that combines the best characteristics of both animals.

    eugenic, *adj.*;   **eugenical**, *adj.*;   **eugenicist**, *n.*

14. **euphemism**   (yōō´ fə mĭz´ əm)   [*pheme* <G. "speech," "saying"]
    n. The use of a neutral, mild, or vague word or phrase instead of a more explicit one that might offend.

    Rather than state directly that someone has died, many people use **euphemisms** like "passed away" and "entered into rest."

    euphemistic, *adj.*;   **euphemize**, *v.*

    NOTA BENE: As circumlocutions for "touchy" subjects, euphemisms can provide unintended, verbose irony. The government is notorious for euphemisms like *strategic misrepresentation* for *lying* or *temporary interruption of an economic expansion* for *recession.* When businesses must lay off employees because of *negative cash flow* (i.e., losses), they may euphemistically call it a *career alternative enhancement program* or *negative employee retention.*

15. **euphony** (yoo′ fə nē) [*phone* <G. "sound"]
    n. Pleasant sounds, especially in spoken language.

    Lullabies in all languages are characterized
    by **euphony**, usually using alliteration of soft
    sounds like *m*, *n*, and *s*.

    euphonic, *adj.*; **euphonious**, *adj.*
    Antonym: **cacophony**

EXERCISE 13A   Circle the letter of the best SYNONYM for the word(s) in bold-faced type.

1. the discovery of a **bonanza**   a. benevolent tribe   b. source of wealth   c. new cure   d. carte blanche   e. potpourri
2. to express it **euphemistically**   a. more politely   b. more bluntly   c. hypocritically   d. articulately   e. more lucidly
3. a decision based on **aesthetic considerations**   a. ethical grounds   b. practical matters   c. artistic taste   d. legal judgments   e. arbitrary whims
4. a noted **eugenicist**   a. pugilist   b. anthropologist   c. aesthete   d. person who studies environmental improvement   e. person who studies improvement of offspring
5. offensive to a(n) **aesthete**   a. artist   b. weakling   c. person with refined tastes   d. poet   e. necromancer
6. to respond **beatifically**   a. mysteriously   b. transcendentally   c. falsely   d. blissfully   e. with great surprise
7. to offer **benign** advice   a. aesthetic   b. palliative   c. obtrusive   d. sympathetic   e. ponderous
8. cultivate a(n) **debonair** manner   a. unsophisticated   b. innocent   c. worldly   d. rural   e. impecunious
9. a **benignant** gesture   a. guilty   b. remorseful   c. careless   d. generous   e. thoughtful
10. to regard as a **boon**   a. friend   b. benefit   c. burden   d. dynamo   e. paragon

Circle the letter of the best ANTONYM for the word(s) in bold-faced type.

11. to create **euphony**   a. acrimony   b. an interregnum   c. cacophony   d. beatitude   e. jealousy
12. a(n) **bona fide** representative   a. illegitimate   b. egregious   c. presumed   d. elected   e. typical

13. likely to appeal to **bons vivants**   a. aesthetes   b. ascetics
    c. pugilists   d. malefactors   e. interlopers
14. to regard as a(n) **benison**   a. dynamo   b. archaism   c. icon
    d. boon   e. anathema

EXERCISE 13B   Circle the letter of the sentence in which the word in bold-faced type is used incorrectly.

1. a. Sir Gawain's bride, the "loathly lady," asks him to choose between the **boon** of having her faithful or the **boon** of having her beautiful.
   b. Marianne North's artistic talent was a **boon** to her career as a botanist, enabling her to paint rare species she found in inaccessible areas of Asia, Africa, and South America.
   c. Although the Soviet Union and the United States were allies during World War II, they later became **boon** opponents.
   d. *Our Hearts Were Young and Gay* recalls adventures in Paris of the youthful Cornelia Otis Skinner and her **boon** companion Emily Kimbrough.
2. a. When Prince Siddhartha attained Nirvana, the highest state of **beatitude**, he became known as the Buddha, which means "the enlightened one."
   b. One of the **Beatitudes** is "Blessed are they that mourn, for they shall be comforted."
   c. Many Americans take a **beatitude** toward government, not even bothering to vote.
   d. Although Dorothea Brooke expects her marriage to Mr. Casaubon to result in **beatitude**, she is bitterly disappointed to find him a self-important pedant.
3. a. Everyone was relieved when the laboratory reported that the tumor was **benign**.
   b. Observing Lady Macbeth's sleepwalking, the doctor remarks that her illness is spiritual rather than physical and she needs the help of a **benign**, not a physician.
   c. Let's try to solve this problem in the morning; a good night's sleep may have a **benign** effect on both of us.
   d. English cottage gardens are characterized by **benign** neglect, with plants sprawling in a natural disorder.
4. a. Boulders of pure gold were discovered during the early days of the Australian **bonanza** of 1851.
   b. A **bonanza** to anthropologists, the Olduvai Gorge in East Africa has produced the earliest examples of humanoid remains.
   c. You can save quite a **bonanza** by turning in your bottles and aluminum cans for recycling.

             d. Using clues from a rare golden scarab and a secretly encoded manuscript, William Legrand discovers a **bonanza**, the buried treasure of Captain Kidd.

EXERCISE 13C   Fill in each blank with the most appropriate word(s) from Lesson 13. Use a word or any of its forms only once.

  1. Dentists and physicians are required to display their diplomas and licenses as evidence that they are _____ medical practitioners.

  2. According to the Koran, those who lose their lives defending Islam die in a state of _____ and directly enter paradise.

  3. The German ministry of health under the Nazis implemented an egregious policy of _____, recommending that people with severe congenital disorders be sterilized.

  4. Citing her motto, "Earnest women can do anything," Josephine St. Pierre Ruffin organized clubs of _____ middle-class matrons who offered assistance to less fortunate families.

  5. Each Friday evening the mother in an observant Jewish family lights the sabbath candles while saying a traditional

     _____.

  6. The Gothic sculptures of saints and angels on the façade of Reims Cathedral are famous for their _____ smiles.

  7. Although well known as a gregarious _____ who delighted in a good party, Diego Rivera was also a tireless worker who created thousands of paintings and murals.

  8. Both the imagery and musical _____ of Keats's ode "To Autumn" capture the sensuous beauty of the "Season of mists and mellow fruitfulness."

  9. In September seniors hope they will appear _____ to impressionable new freshmen.

10. Japanese cuisine gives great attention to the _____ presentation of food, arranging it artfully on a suitable dish with complementary colors and textures.

11. Reports of military action (i.e., warfare) frequently use

     _____ such as *accidental delivery of ordnance equipment* for *bombing the wrong target* and *arbitrary deprivation of life* for *killing*.

EXERCISE 13D   Replace the word or phrase in italics with a key word (or any of its forms) from Lesson 13.

Novels about "coming of age" portray a young person's education in the ways of the world. These works usually record the protagonist's youthful errors of judgment, such as David Copperfield's misplaced trust in his (1) *jovial* companion Steerforth or Elizabeth Bennet's attraction to Mr. Wickham, a predatory (2) *luxury-loving person* in *Pride and Prejudice.* Often the hero affects some inappropriate role, such as Holden Caulfield's attempts to appear (3) *sophisticated and suave* in *The Catcher in the Rye* or Maggie Tulliver's efforts to gain (4) *a state of extreme happiness* through suffering in *The Mill on the Floss.* Often a mentor provides a (5) *kind and helpful* influence, such as Berenice, the confidante of the confused young Frankie in *The Member of the Wedding,* or a(n) (6) *unanticipated lucky break* rescues the protagonist from financial or social ruin. These experiences ultimately lead the protagonists to a realization of their true nature, such as Hanno Buddenbrook's recognition that as a(n) (7) *lover of artistic beauty* he will never find acceptance in his practical, bourgeois family, or Eugene Gant's discovery in *Look Homeward, Angel* that he is a (8) *truly talented and committed* writer.

1. _____   5. _____
2. _____   6. _____
3. _____   7. _____
4. _____   8. _____

LESSON 14

Non ignara mali, miseris succurrere disco.
Not ignorant of distress, I have learned to comfort the unfortunate.—VIRGIL

Key Words

emendation	malaise	malign
illicit	malapropism	malinger
impeccable	malefactor	mendacious
licentious	malevolent	mendicant
maladroit	malfeasance	peccadillo

Familiar Words
maladaptation
maladjustment
malady
malaria
malediction
malfunction
malice
malignant
malnutrition
malodorous
maltreatment

Challenge Words
mala fide
malapropos
maleficence
malversation

MALE <L. "badly," "ill"
MALUS <L. "bad"

1. **maladroit** (măl´ ə droit´) [*adroit* <French *à droite*, "on the right"] *adj.* 1. Clumsy, especially in using the hands.

John Frederick Nim's **maladroit** lover, "whose hands shipwreck vases, / At whose quick touch all glasses chip and ring," receives an unusual tribute in his "Love Poem."

2. Socially clumsy; tactless.

Despite Aunt Ida's **maladroit** efforts to express her affections, readers of *A Yellow Raft in Blue Water* come to recognize her as the emotional center of the family.

maladroitness, *n.*

2. **malaise** (mə lāz´)
n. A vague feeling of ill health or depression.

The squire had attributed his **malaise** to Scotland's gloomy weather, but, in fact, he had the flu.

3. **malapropism** (măl´ ə prŏp´ ĭs əm)
n. The misuse of a word, especially when unintentional, with comic effect.

Gib Lewis, a Texas politician, is famous for his legislative **malapropisms** such as "This is unparalyzed in the state's history" and "[T]hank . . . you for having extinguished yourselves this session."

NOTA BENE: The eponym of *malapropism* is Mrs. Malaprop, a character in Richard Brinsley Sheridan's play *The Rivals* (1775). Sheridan based her name on the French phrase *mal à propos*, "unsuitable for the purpose," because this would-be sophisticate tries "to deck her dull chat with hard words which she don't understand" to hilarious effect. For example, Mrs. Malaprop exhorts her lovesick niece, "Promise to forget this fellow—to illiterate him, I say, quite from memory."

4. **malefactor** (măl´ ə făk´ tər)
[*facere* <L. "to make," "to do"]
n. Someone who commits a crime; an evildoer.

In *Crime and Punishment* Fyodor Dostoevski is less concerned with crime or punishment than with the moral redemption of the **malefactor** Raskolnikov.

malefaction, *n.*
Antonym: **benefactor**

5. **malevolent**   (mǎ lěv′ ə lənt)
    [*velle* <L. "to will," "to wish"]
    adj. Wishing harm to someone; malicious.

    A jinni, an unpredictable supernatural being
    from Muslim legends, can be either
    benevolent or **malevolent**.

    malevolence, *n.*
    Antonym: **benevolent**

6. **malign**   (mə līn′)
    v. To speak harmful untruths about someone or something; to
    traduce.

    "One had rather **malign** oneself than not speak of oneself at all."
    —François, Duc de la Rochefoucauld

    adj. Showing an evil disposition; intending harm or evil.

    Hannah Arendt's study of evil has shown that most cruelty results not
    from **malign** intentions but from unwillingness to prevent wrongdoing.

    maligner, *n.*

7. **malfeasance**   (mǎl fē′ zəns)   [*facere* <L. "to make," "to do"]
    n. Misconduct, especially by a public official.

    During the presidency of Warren G. Harding, Harry M. Daugherty, the
    U.S. attorney general, and his cronies in the "Ohio Gang" garnered
    more than three hundred million dollars through **malfeasance**, accepting
    bribes for public offices, land and oil reserves, and judgeships.

    NOTA BENE: Legal language distinguishes among acts of wrongdoing.
    Malfeasance is illegal conduct by a person in authority. Improper per-
    formance of some otherwise lawful act (for example, medical malprac-
    tice) is termed *malfeasance*. On the other hand, *nonfeasance* describes a
    sin of omission, or failure to do what law or duty requires (for exam-
    ple, sleeping while on guard).

8. **malinger**   (mə lǐng′ gər)
    intr. v. To pretend to be sick or injured in
    order to evade responsibilities.

    Shel Silverstein's poem "Sick" describes
    a child determined to **malinger** until she
    discovers that it is Saturday.

    malingerer, *n.*

Familiar Word
mend

MENDUM <L. "fault," "defect"

9. **mendacious** (měn dā′ shəs)
adj. Lying; untruthful; false.

The Food and Drug Administration prohibits pharmaceutical companies from making **mendacious** allegations about a medication.

mendacity, *n.*
Antonym: **veracious**

Challenge Word
mendicity

10. **mendicant** (měn′ dĭ kənt)
n. A beggar; anyone who earns a living by begging.

Forbidden to own more than their robes, rosary, and a bowl for begging food, Buddhist monks are **mendicants** who depend entirely on the generosity of the community for their food.

mendicancy, *n.*; **mendicant**, *adj.*

11. **emendation** (ĭ měn dā′ shən, ē měn dā′ shən)
[*e* = *ex* <L. "from," "out of"]
n. Alteration or improvement of writing to remove errors.

For centuries textual scholars have tried to make plausible **emendations** of the few surviving fragments of Sappho's poetry.

emend, *v.*; **emendate**, *v.*; **emendatory**, *adj.*;
emender, *n.*

Challenge Words
peccable
peccancy
peccant
peccavi

PECCATUM <L. "sin," "crime," "offense," "fault"

12. **peccadillo** (pěk′ ə dĭl′ ō)
[-*illo* <Spanish diminutive]
n. A small sin or fault; a trifling offense.

While Daisy Miller dismisses her unchaperoned moonlight walk in the Colosseum as an innocent **peccadillo**, the British community in Rome regards her comportment as scandalous.

13. **impeccable** (ĭm pĕk′ ə bəl)   [*im* = *in* <L. "not"]
    adj. Without flaw; faultless.

    Once Henry Higgins trains Eliza Doolittle to speak with an **impeccable** aristocratic accent, the Cockney flower seller can pass for a duchess.

<table>
<tr><td>

Familiar Words
leisure
license

</td></tr>
</table>

LICENTIA <L. "freedom"

14. **licentious** (lī sĕn′ shəs)
    adj. Lacking moral discipline or self-restraint, especially in sexual matters.

    "My English text is chaste, and all **licentious** passages are left in the obscurity of a learned language."—Edward Gibbon

    licentiousness, *n.*

15. **illicit** (ĭ lĭs′ ĭt)   [*il* = *in* <L. "not"]
    adj. Illegal; not sanctioned by law or tradition.

    Dante meets the notorious **illicit** lovers Paolo and Francesca in the second circle of hell where "sinners of the flesh" are confined.

    illicitness, *n.*
    Antonym: **licit**

EXERCISE 14A

Circle the letter of the best SYNONYM for the word in bold-faced type.

1. suspected **malfeasance**   a. mendacity   b. necromancy
   c. apostasy   d. malignancy   e. misconduct
2. the author's **emended** text   a. corrected   b. summarized
   c. expunged   d. analyzed   e. impugned
3. a hilarious **malapropism**   a. emendation   b. misuse of a word
   c. hypothesis   d. elucidation   e. adumbration
4. with **impeccable** courtesy   a. perfect   b. hypocritical
   c. egregious   d. unnatural   e. impossible
5. accused of **malingering**   a. loitering   b. maligning
   c. pretending to be friendly   d. faking illness   e. lying
6. guilty of a **peccadillo**   a. crime   b. malfeasance   c. petty
   offense   d. malefaction   e. gross impropriety
7. **illicit** business dealings   a. profitable   b. explicit   c. implicit
   d. out-moded   e. unlawful
8. such **maladroit** behavior   a. awkward   b. benign   c. beatific
   d. decadent   e. pugnacious
9. to anticipate **mendicancy**   a. honesty   b. depreciation
   c. beggary   d. philanthropy   e. subjectivity

Circle the letter of the best ANTONYM for the word in bold-faced type.

10. an occasional **malefactor**   a. dynamo   b. paragon   c. bon vivant   d. mendicant   e. recidivist
11. a continuing **malaise**   a. illness   b. elucidation   c. dislike d. adumbration   e. sense of well-being
12. a reputation for **licentiousness**   a. self-restraint   b. decadence c. legal expertise   d. sensitivity   e. illicitness

EXERCISE 14B   Circle the letter of the sentence in which the word in bold-faced type is used incorrectly.

1. a. The explosion of the U.S. space shuttle *Challenger* was attributed to a **malevolent** valve in the fuel line.
    b. Self-interest, not **malevolence**, leads Madame Merle to deceive Isabel Archer.
    c. You have mistaken her nearsighted squint for a **malevolent** glare.
    d. Although she possesses incriminating letters with which she could blackmail Bertha Dorset and regain her own social position, Lily Bart refuses to act so **malevolently**.
2. a. Occasionally a fine physician is too **maladroit** to become a surgeon.
    b. Don't expect me to dance! I'm so **maladroit** that I feel as though I have two left feet.
    c. In *Tootsie* Dustin Hoffman plays a male actor who at first **maladroitly** poses as a woman but gradually perfects the role.
    d. Too socially **maladroit** to host a sophisticated dance, Mick Kelly abandons her guests to play street games with the neighborhood children.
3. a. To correct his **maligned** teeth, he wore a retainer at night.
    b. Even Ellen Olenska's **maligners** must admit that she is beautiful and intelligent.
    c. Voters were appalled as the candidates began to **malign** each other with increasing acrimony.
    d. During the cold war, the United States Department of State suspected every Soviet initiative of harboring some **malign** intention.

EXERCISE 14C   Matching: On the line at the left, write the letter of the negative behavior
that best matches the noun.

_____	**1.** peccadillo	A. "murdering" the language
_____	**2.** malefaction	B. telling a little white lie
_____	**3.** malevolence	C. begging for spare change
_____	**4.** malfeasance	D. dropping a plate at the buffet
_____	**5.** mendacity	E. hoping someone breaks a leg
_____	**6.** licentiousness	F. holding up a stage coach
_____	**7.** malapropism	G. telling a gross untruth
_____	**8.** mendicancy	H. making unwelcome sexual overtures
_____	**9.** illicitness	I. capturing endangered species
_____	**10.** maladroitness	J. selling public property for personal profit

EXERCISE 14D   Replace the word or phrase in italics with a key word (or any of its forms)
from Lesson 14. Some words may be used more than once.

Whenever she wrote something, Virginia Woolf suffered a (1) *feeling
of discomfort* because her work seemed inadequate to her. In her need to
make every page (2) *without imperfection,* she made continual (3) *alterations
to remove errors* in what she had written. What might seem to others a literary (4) *trifling fault* seemed to her a serious debasement of her writing.
As a result of this constant rewriting, almost everything she published is of
uniformly excellent quality.

1. _____   3. _____

2. _____   4. _____

Once (5) *falsely discredited* as the "yuppie flu," Chronic Fatigue
Syndrome has now been acknowledged by the Centers for Disease Control
and Prevention as a bona fide illness. Victims suffered not only its physical
symptoms such as fever, loss of energy, and (6) *vague feelings of depression,*
but also endured accusations that they were (7) *lying* hypochondriacs who
were (8) *making up disabilities to avoid work.* Now scientists are seriously
researching the cause of this mysterious malady.

5. _____   7. _____

6. _____   8. _____

REVIEW EXERCISES FOR LESSONS 13 AND 14

1 Circle the letter of the best answer to the following analogies and questions about roots and definitions.

1. maladroit : clumsy : :
   a. benign : malign
   b. benignant : kindly
   c. euphonious : cacophonous
   d. licentious : liberal
   e. aesthetic : athletic
2. peccadillo : treason : :
   a. bonanza : abatement
   b. impunity : euphemism
   c. malapropism : Mrs. Malaprop
   d. hint : proclamation
   e. euphony : symphony
3. Which word has no "good" in it?
   a. Benedict   b. bonbon   c. bounty   d. bench   e. eulogy
4. Which word has no "bad" in it?
   a. malaria   b. malediction   c. mallet   d. malpractice   e. malady
5. Which root is defined incorrectly?
   a. *aisthanesthai* <G. "beauty"
   b. *eu* <G. "good"
   c. *mendum* <L. "defect"
   d. *peccatum* <L. "sin"
   e. *licentia* <L. "freedom"

2 Completions: Circle the letter of the pair of words that best completes the meaning of each sentence.

1. Although _____ like to live luxuriously, they are not necessarily _____ people who lack moral self-restraint.
   a. aesthetes . . . malevolent
   b. interlopers . . . illicit
   c. oligarchs . . . politic
   d. bons vivants . . . licentious
   e. pugilists . . . puissant
2. With his top hat and _____ tuxedo, the dancer Fred Astaire epitomized for American movie-goers the _____ cosmopolite.
   a. beatific . . . euphonious
   b. punctilious . . . benign
   c. decadent . . . maladroit
   d. aesthetic . . . reclusive
   e. impeccable . . . debonair

3. My teacher suggested some ways to _____ my sonnet, making it more _____ without losing any of its original meaning.
   a. malign . . . pungent
   b. emend . . . euphonious
   c. pall . . . impeccable
   d. occlude . . . apocryphal
   e. concede . . . bona fide

4. When poverty forced him to become a_____, he never lost his _____ sensibilities and continued to write about the beauties of nature around him.
   a. boon . . . debonair
   b. peccadillo . . . mendacious
   c. mendicant . . . aesthetic
   d. recluse . . . compunctious
   e. belligerent . . . benign

5. Although most people dismissed as _____ Anastasia's claims that she was the only surviving daughter of Czar Nicholas II, the former Czar's mother regarded her as a(n) _____ member of the Romanov family.
   a. mendacious . . . bona fide
   b. euphony . . . benign
   c. benignant . . . illicit
   d. impeccable . . . malign
   e. predatory . . . punctilious

6. Suffering from a general _____ after long months of winter cold and dark, they enjoyed the _____ warmth of the spring sunshine.
   a. depredation . . . benignant
   b. beatitude . . . pungent
   c. peccadillo . . . forte
   d. recidivism . . . aesthetic
   e. malaise . . . benign

7. In addition to "forty-niners" hoping to strike it rich from the _____ of gold discovered in California, the gold rush also attracted _____ hoping to rob and cheat the prospectors.
   a. benison . . . pugilists
   b. boon . . . necromancers
   c. bonanza . . . malefactors
   d. beatitude . . . pungent
   e. potpourri . . . malapropisms

3 Fill in each blank with the most appropriate word from Lessons 13 and 14. Use a word or any of its forms only once.

The temples of Angkor Wat rank among the architectural treasures of the world. Built between the 9th and 14th centuries, they mark the zenith of the Khmer culture of Cambodia in both political power and

a) _____ (artistic) accomplishment. Each of the nearly one hundred temples is laid out with

b) _____ (flawless) symmetry, including outer walls and courtyards, formal gateways, and a central "mountain temple," all covered with carved images of rulers, demons, and

c) _____ (joyful or blessed) figures from Buddhist and Hindu mythology.

However, in recent years a(n) d) _____ (illegal) trade in Khmer antiquities has turned this world treasure into

a(n) e) _____ (unexpected source of money) for thieves. These local f) _____s (criminals) enter the unguarded temples at night and use crude tools to behead statues and remove bas-reliefs. For every priceless piece they manage to

carry away, their g) _____ (clumsy) techniques leave four or five others in ruins.

Responsibility for this vandalism rests less on the thieves, most of whom are both ignorant of the value of these works of art and desperately

poor, than on the h) _____ (genuine, recognized) art dealers of Europe and North America who receive

them. Fully conscious of their own i) _____ (misconduct), they label these stolen Khmer treasures with the

j) _____ (neutral phrase) "origin unknown" and sell them at great profit.

4 Writing or Discussion Activities

1. Classified Advertisements
   Because newspapers generally charge by the word for the classified advertisements, they should be as brief as possible. Rewrite the following advertisements, replacing the numbered words and phrases with a key word from Lessons 13 and 14 and condensing the whole message as much as possible.

a. A (1) *worldly sophisticated* (2) *person with a refined appreciation of beauty* wants to rent a quiet retreat in the country in order to recover from a (3) *vague feeling of depression*.

b. The (4) *criminal offender* who stole a dog has discovered it to be (5) *intending him harm* and excessively eager for a fight and would now be extremely thankful if the (6) *honest-to-goodness* owner would claim the beast.

c. Here's a real (7) *stroke of good luck*: a person who edits for a living offers (8) *to remove the mistakes from* what you write so you can turn in (9) *error-free* reports and letters.

d. Parents want their runaway child to know that they forgive all the (10) *little trifling offenses* of the past. They realize that they handled the situation in a (11) *socially clumsy and tactless* way. They urge their child to come home for their (12) *blessing*.

e. A (13) *person who loves food and drink* would be in a state of (14) *exalted happiness* if the mysterious unknown person accosted at last weekend's party would (15) *graciously and sympathetically* understand that nothing (16) *lacking in moral discipline* was intended. Please pick up the telephone and call.

2. Shakespeare says "there is nothing either good or bad but thinking makes it so." Describe a person from two perspectives, first from the point of view of someone who regards that person as benign, then from the point of view of someone who regards him or her as malign.

3. Everyone uses euphemisms on occasion to express what seems awkward or embarrassing. Create a euphemistic way to convey these difficult statements.

   a. I have to fire you because of your continual malingering.
   b. After dinner at your house I had food poisoning.
   c. Since you ask, that new outfit makes you look ridiculous.
   d. I don't want to go out with you.
   e. Your proposed plan will never work.

The Law

LESSON 15

Nemo me impune lacessit.
No one provokes me with impunity.—Motto of the Crown of Scotland

Key Words		
allege	legate	reproof
approbation	probity	subpoena
censorious	punitive	vendetta
censure	relegate	vindicate
impunity	reprobate	vindictive

Familiar Words
censor
censorship
census

Challenge Word
recension

CENSEO, CENSERE, CENSUI, CENSUM <L. "to give an opinion," "to estimate"
CENSOR, CENSORIS <L. "a magistrate," "a severe judge," "a rigid moralist"

1. **censorious** (sĕn sōr′ ē əs, sĕn sôr′ ē əs)
   adj. Faultfinding; severely critical.

   When Maggie Tulliver's **censorious** aunts find fault with her thick, dark hair, the wounded child cuts it all off.

   censoriousness, *n.*

2. **censure** (sĕn′ shər)
   tr. v. To criticize harshly.

"Mankind **censures** injustice, fearing that they may be the victims of it and not because they shrink from committing it."—Plato

censure, n.

NOTA BENE: *Consensus,* "agreement," comes from the Latin verb *sentire,* "to feel," and is consequently spelled with an *s* after the prefix.

LEGO, LEGARE, LEGAVI, LEGATUM
<L. "to commission," "to send"

Familiar Words
colleague
delegate
legacy

Challenge Words
legatee
legator

3. **legate** (lĕg' ĭt)
   n. A representative sent on a special mission, especially one representing the pope.

   A papal **legate** traveled from Rome to hear Martin Luther bring charges against the Catholic church before the Diet of Worms.

   legation, *n.*

4. **allege** (ə lĕj') [*al* = *ad* <L. "to," "toward"]
   tr. v. To claim that something is true without necessarily having proof; to advance as an argument or excuse.

   Since a person is presumed innocent until proven guilty, newspaper reports say "Witnesses **allege** that they saw the accused" rather than "Witnesses say that they saw the criminal."

   allegation, *n.*; **allegedly**, *adv.*

5. **relegate** (rĕl' ə gāt) [*re* <L. "back," "again"]
   tr. v. To banish to a place of exile; to dismiss to an obscure or inferior position.

   Refusing to be **relegated** to the "women's pages," Dorothy Thompson, the first American woman to head a foreign news bureau, reported so forcefully on the rise of Hitler that she also became the first American journalist to be expelled from Germany.

   relegation, *n.*

POENA <L. "penalty," "punishment"
PUNIO, PUNIRE, PUNIVI, PUNITUM <L. "to punish"

Familiar Words
pain
penal
penalize
pine
punish

6. **punitive** (pyōō' nə tĭv)
   adj. Inflicting or intending punishment.

   Because the Communist regime regarded kulaks as class enemies, these well-to-do Russian peasants suffered **punitive** relocation to Siberia.

   punitiveness, *n.*

7. **impunity**   (ĭm pyōō′ nə tē)   [*im* = *in* <L. "not"]
   n. Exemption from punishment or penalty, as a result of a particular act.

During the medieval Feast of Fools, now our April Fool's Day, servants could mock their employers with **impunity**.

NOTA BENE: Although *impugn* and *impunity* may look and sound like relatives, *impugn* is derived from the root *pugnare*, meaning "to fight," while *impunity* is derived from *poena*.

8. **subpoena**   (sə pē′ nə)   [*sub* <L. "under"]
   n. A legal requirement that someone or something appear in court to give or be evidence.

When Archibald Cox, the special prosecutor for the Watergate affair, issued a **subpoena** for the recorded telephone conversations of President Richard Nixon, the president responded by firing him.

subpoena, *tr. v.*

PROBO, PROBARE, PROBAVI, PROBATUM
<L. "to prove," "to test," "to approve"

9. **probity**   (prō′ bə tē)
   n. Impeccable integrity; uprightness.

> Look at the peace of inanimate things,
> The sanity of the stones,
> The **probity** of pasture fields, dead trees,
> Old hills, and patient bones.—T. H. White

10. **approbation**   (ăp rə bā′ shən)
    [*ap* = *ad* <L. "to," "toward"]
    n. Praise; commendation; official approval.

"Even when we are quite alone, how often do we think with pleasure or pain of what others think of us—of their imagined **approbation** or disapprobation."—Charles Darwin

approbate, *v.*; **approbative**, *adj.*; **approbatory**, *adj.*
Antonym: **disapprobation**

11. **reprobate**   (rĕp′ rə bāt′)   [*re* <L. "back," "again"]
    n. A morally decadent person.

Realizing that he has found love and forgiveness for his misdeeds, Michael Henchard declares, "Who is such a **reprobate** as I! And yet it seems that even I be in Somebody's hand!"

reprobate, *adj.*; **reprobate**, *v.*; **reprobation**, *n.*

12. **reproof** (rĭ prōōf′)
    [*re* <L. "back," "again"]
    n. An expression of criticism for a fault or
    misdeed; a scolding.

    Despite her mother's bitter **reproof** of her
    "mad determination to study medicine,"
    Anne Walter Fearn became a physician in
    1893 and served as a missionary doctor
    in China.

    reprovable, *adj.*; **reprove**, *v.*; **reprover**, *n.*

<table>
<tr><td>

Familiar Words
avenge
revenge
vengeance
vengeful

</td></tr>
</table>

VINDICO, VINDICARE, VINDICAVI, VINDICATUM
<L. "to avenge"

13. **vindicate** (vĭn dĭ kāt′)
    tr. v. To clear from blame; to exonerate; to prove to be valid.

    "History has a long-range perspective. It ultimately passes stern judg-
    ments on tyrants and **vindicates** those who fought . . . against political
    oppression. . . ."—Elizabeth Gurley Flynn

    vindicable, *adj.*; **vindication**, *n.*; **vindicator**, *n.*; **vindicatory**, *adj.*

14. **vindictive** (vĭn dĭk′ tĭv)
    adj. Revengeful; unforgiving.

    "It is not true that suffering enobles
    the character; happiness does that
    sometimes, but suffering, for the most
    part, makes men petty and **vindictive**."
    —William Somerset Maugham

    vindictiveness, *n.*

15. **vendetta** (věn dět′ ə)
    n. A bitter feud, especially one perpetuated by acts of revenge, often
    between successive generations of two families or clans.

    Despite the fierce **vendetta** raging between the Doone clan and the
    people of Oare parish, whose leading family is the Ridds, Lorna Doone
    and John Ridd fall in love and marry.

EXERCISE 15A   Circle the letter of the best SYNONYM for the word in bold-faced type.

1. to send a(n) **legation**   a. subpoena   b. group with a special mission   c. vindictive message   d. allegation   e. letter that demands a reply
2. to expect a(n) **vendetta**   a. ambush   b. subpoena   c. allegation   d. vengeful feud   e. altercation
3. to fear a(n) **subpoena**   a. consensus   b. censorious judge   c. underhanded trick   d. ban   e. summons to court
4. a reputation for **probity**   a. mendacity   b. apostasy   c. inquisitiveness   d. rectitude   e. persistence
5. deserving **reproof**   a. evidence   b. censorship   c. impunity   d. castigation   e. to be proved again
6. despite their **relegation**   a. vindication   b. reclusion   c. banishment   d. impunity   e. depredation
7. to find a(n) **vindicator**   a. apologist   b. malefactor   c. scapegoat   d. accuser   e. iconoclast
8. to respond with **censoriousness**   a. warm approval   b. malevolence   c. harsh criticism   d. a diatribe   e. punctiliousness
9. to gain their **approbation**   a. esteem   b. emendation   c. reproof   d. permission   e. malaise

Circle the letter of the best ANTONYM for the word in bold-faced type.

10. intentionally **punitive**   a. aesthetic   b. vindicative   c. malign   d. unjust   e. rewarding
11. known for her **reprobation**   a. mendacity   b. impunity   c. debonair manner   d. probity   e. carelessness
12. obvious **vindictiveness**   a. defeat   b. approbation   c. forgiveness   d. beatitude   e. malignance
13. to expect **impunity**   a. fame   b. a reward   c. punishment   d. an altercation   e. pecuniary appreciation

EXERCISE 15B   Circle the letter of the sentence in which the word in bold-faced type is used incorrectly.

1. a. The **allegation** that Nero, a would-be musician, fiddled while Rome burned is almost certainly apocryphal.
    b. Following the shooting of President John F. Kennedy, witnesses **alleged** that they heard shots coming from more than one direction.
    c. Idolized by admirers too young to have seen him in person, Elvis Presley has become **alleged** years after his death.
    d. Sarah Woodruff encourages the harmful **allegation** that she is the licentious "French lieutenant's woman" in order to liberate herself from Victorian social expectations.

2. a. Emma finally realizes that she loves Mr. Knightley, the only person who has ever **reproved** her for her meddlesome behavior.
   b. Even when manufacturers produce years of convincing research, the Food and Drug Administration must **reprove** a medicine in its own laboratories before approving it for sale.
   c. Despite **reproof**, Amelia Jenks Bloomer continued to publicize billowly pantaloons for women because they were more practical than fashionable hoopskirts and trains.
   d. Although Blanche DuBois's lies and heavy drinking are **reprovable**, the audience nevertheless sympathizes with her futile idealism.

3. a. Ralph Waldo Emerson **censured** Jane Austen as "vulgar in tone, sterile in artistic invention . . . without genius, wit, or knowledge of the world."
   b. In Amish communities the most extreme form of **censure** is shunning, when even family members may not speak to the person being chastened.
   c. Many formerly Communist countries in Eastern Europe established a state **censure** who had responsibility for banning "dangerous" publications.
   d. The United Nations formally **censured** the Republic of South Africa for its racist policy of apartheid.

EXERCISE 15C

Fill in each blank with the most appropriate word from Lesson 15. Use a word or any of its forms only once.

1. J. Enoch Powell opposed Britain's entry into the Common Market, declaring that such a union would not have "the willing

   _____ and consent of the nation."

2. A person who has officially received a(n) _____ but willingly fails to appear in court or turn over required documents is guilty of contempt of court, a criminal offense.

3. In ironic response to the _____ of reviewers who found his shows vulgar, the millionaire pianist Liberace said, "I cried all the way to the bank."

4. The drama critic, known for her _____ reviews, could find nothing uncomplimentary to say about this new play.

5. In 1838 the people of the Cherokee Nation were forcibly removed from their rich lands in Tennessee and North Carolina, sent on a forced march known as the Trail of Tears, and

   _____ to arid regions in Oklahoma.

6. Upholding the principle that the law should not be

   _____, the legal scholar William Blackstone said, "It is better that ten guilty persons escape than one innocent suffer."

7. On her election as president of the United Nations General Assembly, Vijayalakshmi Pandit declared that she would disassociate

   herself from the Indian _____ to the UN and discharge her duties with complete impartiality.

EXERCISE 15D   Replace the word or phrase in italics with a key word (or any of its forms) from Lesson 15.

A legendary (1) *family feud* between the Hatfields and the McCoys took place in the mountains of Kentucky. Living beyond the reach of the law, the two families staged a private war with seeming (2) *exemption from legal consequences.* Some local historians say that the original conflict that began this (3) *vengefulness* was competition in the illicit whiskey trade; others (4) *claim without proof* that the problem was illicit love.

1. _____   3. _____

2. _____   4. _____

The story of Susanna and the elders found in the Apocrypha illustrates how a young wife's (5) *integrity* is (6) *cleared from blame* by a wise judge. Falsely accused of adultery by two (7) *revengeful* (8) *morally corrupt old men* who spy on her while she is bathing, Susanna receives the (9) *harshly punishing* sentence of death by stoning. The prophet Daniel intercedes, however, finds the elders' (10) *unsupported claims* to be false, and condemns them instead.

5. _____   8. _____

6. _____   9. _____

7. _____   10. _____

LESSON 16

De minimus non curat lex.
The law doesn't care about trifles.

Key Words

abjure	arbitrate	judicious
abrogate	arrogate	perjury
adjudicate	conjure	prerogative
adjure	exhort	rogue
arbitrary	hortatory	surrogate

Challenge Words
arbiter
arbitrable
arbitrage
arbitrament

ARBITER <L. "judge," "witness," "spectator"
ARBITROR, ARBITRARI, ARBITRATUM
<L. "to hear," "to perceive"

1. **arbitrary**   (är′ bə trĕr′ ē)
    adj. Based on a subjective whim or random choice.

    "Those who won our independence believed that. . . [in] government the deliberate forces should prevail over the **arbitrary**."—Louis Dembitz Brandeis

    arbitrariness, *n.*

2. **arbitrate**   (är′ bə trāt′)
    tr. v. To judge or decide in the manner of an umpire or person granted power to make a decision.

    To **arbitrate** a dispute between two women who claimed the same baby, King Solomon ordered that it be cut in half, whereupon the true mother dropped her claim in order to save the baby's life.

    arbitration, *n.*; **arbitrator**, *n.*

HORTOR, HORTARI, HORTATUM <L. "to urge,"
"to encourage"

3. **hortatory**   (hôr′ tə tôr ē)
    adj. Marked by a strong urging to take some action.

    The **hortatory** classical motto adopted for the Olympic Games is *Citius, altius, fortius*, meaning "Swifter, higher, stronger."

4. **exhort**   (ĭg zôrt')   [*ex* <L. "from," "out of"]
   tr. v. To urge, advise, or admonish vigorously.

   Mary Harris ("Mother") Jones, a fiery organizer for the United Mine Workers, **exhorted** women, "No matter what your fight, don't be ladylike."

   exhorter, *n.*; **exhortation**, *n.*; **exhortative**, *adj.*

JUDEX, JUDICIS <L. "judge"
JUDICO, JUDICARE, JUDICAVI, JUDICATUM
<L. "to judge," "to decide"

5. **judicious**   (jōō dĭsh' əs)
   adj. Showing good judgment; sensible.

   "Nothing like a little **judicious** levity."—Robert Louis Stevenson

   judiciousness, *n.*
   Antonym: **injudicious**

6. **adjudicate**   (ə jōō' dĭ kāt')
   [*ad* <L. "to," "toward"]
   tr. v. To settle a case by legal means; to act as a judge.

   Although the World Court **adjudicates** legal disputes between nations, it has no authority to enforce its decisions.

   adjudicative, *adj.*; **adjudication**, *n.*; **adjudicator**, *n.*

JURO, JURARE, JURAVI, JURATUM <L. "to swear," "to take an oath"

7. **abjure**   (ăb jōōr')   [*ab* <L. "away from"]
   tr. v. To renounce formally; to recant.

   In 1654 Queen Christina of Sweden **abjured** the Protestant faith and abdicated her throne to become a Roman Catholic.

   abjuration, *n.*; **abjurer**, *n.*

8. **adjure**   (ə jōōr')   [*ad* <L. "to," "toward"]
   tr. v. To command or urge solemnly.

   Beatrice Fairfax's turn-of-the-century newspaper advice column, "Letters from the Lovelorn," **adjured** her correspondents to "Dry your eyes, roll up your sleeves, and dig for a practical solution."

   adjuration, *n.*; **adjurer, adjuror**, *n.*

9. **conjure** (kŏn′ jər, kən jōōr′)   [*con = cum* <L. "with"]
tr. v. To cause to happen as if by magic; to produce as if from nothing; to stimulate the imagination (often used with *up*).

The two-thousandth performance of the play, with new costumes and a stellar cast, **conjured** up all of the excitement of its opening night.

intr. v. To practice legerdemain; to summon a spirit by magic spell.

Disguised as a boy, Rosalind claims to Orlando that she has the power to **conjure** and can summon his beloved Rosalind for him whenever she likes.

conjurgation, *n.*; **conjurer, conjuror**, *n.*

NOTA BENE: The phrase "a name to conjure with" means "an important or respected name." It can also refer to the holder of the name, as in, Among art lovers, Frida Kahlo is a name to conjure with.

10. **perjury** (pûr′ jə rē)   [*per* <L. "through"]
n. The intentional giving of false evidence or breaking of an oath, especially in a court of law.

"There is nothing so terrible as **perjury**. There is something uncanny and awful about that sin."—Selma Lagerlöf

perjurer, *n.*; **perjurious**, *adj.*

Familiar Words
arrogant
derogatory
interrogate

Challenge Words
corvée
derogate
erogate
prorogue

ROGO, ROGARE, ROGAVI, ROGATUM <L. "to ask," "to beg"

11. **rogue** (rōg)
n. A malicious, unprincipled person; a mountebank.

Regina Giddens proves herself a **rogue**, conniving to extort money from her fatally ill husband and refusing him medicine when he feels an attack coming on.

adj. Something that separates itself from the community or the normal standard, often with harmful results, used especially with natural phenomena; a renegade.

On a calm day a **rogue** wave suddenly washed over the promontory and swept a hiker out to sea.

rogue, *v.*; **roguery**, *n.*; **roguish**, *adj.*

NOTA BENE: A rogue can also be a person who playfully pretends to be wicked. Such mischievous pretense is often accompanied by roguish smiles or roguish remarks and may earn the pretender an affectionate epithet like "You old rogue, you!"

12. **abrogate** (ăb′ rō gāt′) [*ab* <L. "away from"]
tr. v. To abolish or repeal, especially a law.

When new citizens take the oath to defend the United States Constitution, they also swear to "**abrogate** loyalty to prince and potentate."

abrogation, *n.*

13. **arrogate** (ăr′ ə gāt′) [*ar = ad* <L. "to," "toward"]
tr. v. To take or claim without permission or authority.

According to English common law a "squatter" who **arrogates** public land, living on it for seven years and improving it, has some claim to ownership.

arrogation, *n.*; **arrogative**, *adj.*; **arrogator**, *n.*

14. **prerogative** (prĭ rŏg′ ə tĭv) [*pre* <L. "before"]
n. A right or privilege belonging to a particular person, office, or group.

Medical ethicists study issues such as a parent's **prerogative** to refuse medical treatment for a child because of religious reasons even though the child may die as a result.

15. **surrogate** (sûr′ ə gĭt, sûr′ ə gāt) [*sur = sub* <L. "under"]
n. A substitute.

Konrad Lorenz showed that orphaned animals will bond with almost any **surrogate**, in some cases creating ludicrous families such as the flock of geese that followed a large dog as its parent.

surrogate, *adj.*

EXERCISE 16A

Circle the letter of the best SYNONYM for the word in bold-faced type.

1. a(n) **surrogate** leader   a. alleged   b. mendicant   c. bona fide   d. substitute   e. reprobate
2. a parental **prerogative**   a. roguery   b. vendetta   c. privilege   d. impunity   e. hegemony
3. with a(n) **roguish** glance   a. chastened   b. beatific   c. mischievous   d. approbative   e. vindictive
4. repeated **adjurations**   a. entreaties   b. sincere prayers   c. oaths   d. legal battles   e. formal renunciations

5. to act as a(n) **adjudicator**   a. surrogate   b. peacemaker
    c. friend   d subpoena   e. judge
6. a rousing **exhortation**   a. malaproprism   b. admonition
    c. arbitration   d. benison   e. diatribe
7. skilled in **arbitration**   a. winning approbation   b. arrogation
    c. conjuring   d. abrogation   e. making just decisions
8. a solemn **abjuration**   a. renunciation   b. conjuration
    c. annunciation   d. affirmation   e. aggregation
9. acted with **judiciousness**   a. discretion   b. acumen
    c. presumption   d. good judgment   e. impunity
10. to give **perjured** testimony   a. benignant   b. vindictive
    c. punctilious   d. untruthful   e. lucid

Circle the letter of the best ANTONYM for the word in bold-faced type.

11. expected **arbitrariness**   a. decisions based on principles
    b. impunity   c. censoriousness   d. vindictiveness   e. biased
    judgment
12. gave **hortatory** reproof   a. hinting   b. euphemistic   c. illicit
    d. punctilious   e. censorious
13. an unexpected **abrogation**   a. creation of a law   b. breaking
    of a law   c. telling of a lie   d. cancellation of a prerogative
    e. approbation

EXERCISE 16B   Circle the letter of the sentence in which the word in bold-faced type is
used incorrectly.

1. a. Julia Child showed television audiences how to **conjure** up
       elegant French dishes from ordinary American ingredients.
    b. Examining the evidence, the police **conjure** that the murder
       occurred before midnight.
    c. Dr. Faustus **conjures** up the demon Mephistopheles to be his
       servant.
    d. The **conjurer's** expression *hocus pocus* is actually derived from a
       mishearing of *hoc est*, a phrase from the Catholic mass.
2. a. Jacob works for seven years to earn the right to marry Rachel,
       but on the wedding night her sister Leah is **surrogated** for her.
    b. During World War II chicory was often used in Europe as a
       surrogate for coffee.
    c. When President Jimmy Carter was unable to attend an official
       function, his wife Rosalynn Carter often attended as his
       surrogate.
    d. Nana, a Saint Bernard, serves as a **surrogate** mother to the
       Darling children in *Peter Pan*.

3. a. Michel de Montaigne gave this advice to would-be **perjurers**:
       "Unless a man feels he has a good enough memory, he should
       never venture to lie."
    b. Juliet adjures Romeo to be truthful in his declarations of love,
       noting that lovers are inclined to **perjure** themselves.
    c. To prevent **perjurious** testimony, all witnesses must swear that
       they are telling "nothing but the truth."
    d. Before a major crime can be brought to trial, it must first be
       heard by a **perjury** that determines whether sufficient evidence
       exists to make a case.

4. a. As a young police officer in Burma, George Orwell had to shoot
       a dangerous **rogue** elephant that had escaped its owner.
    b. Famous for her **roguish** remarks, Alice Roosevelt Longworth
       once said, "If you haven't got anything good to say about anyone,
       come and sit by me."
    c. The investigative reporting of Ida Tarbell exposed widespread
       roguery in the oil business and led in 1911 to dissolution of the
       Standard Oil Company of New Jersey under the Sherman Anti-
       Trust Act.
    d. When I was five, I was discovered that Santa Claus was only a
       rogue created by my parents.

EXERCISE 16C   Fill in each blank with the most appropriate word from Lesson 16. Use a
word or any of its forms only once.

1. The Roman historian Tacitus described how the wives of Germanic

    warriors stood by the battlefield to _____
    their husbands to deeds of bravery.

2. An American presidential nominee has the _____
    to select a vice-presidential running mate.

3. When Hermia refuses to marry the man her father has selected,
    King Theseus gives her two alternatives, "Either to die the death,

    or to _____ / forever the society of men."

4. Trial by jury, which evolved from the twelfth-century practice of
    appointing twelve people to settle disputes over ownership of land,

    provided an alternative to the more _____
    method of trial by ordeal.

5. In the 1954 case *Brown v. Board of Education*, the Supreme

    Court _____ the practice of segregating
    schools by race.

6. Caroline Norton's 1838 pamphlet, "A Plain Letter,"

    _____ Parliament to recognize that children were not the exclusive property of their fathers.

7. "You that intend to write what is worthy to be read more than once, blot frequently: and take no pains to make the multitude

    admire you, content with a few _____ readers."—Horace

8. In one of the most famous _____ speeches in English literature, Shakespeare's King Henry V urges his army: "Once more into the breach, dear friends, once more, Or close the wall up with our English dead."

9. When her employer _____ the right to rename her because her real name was supposedly too long, young Maya Angelou quit her job in protest.

10. Welcoming once-belligerent Germany to the League of Nations, the French premier Aristide Briand optimistically declared, "Draw back the rifles, draw back the machine guns, the cannons—trust in

    conciliation, in _____, in peace."

EXERCISE 16D   Replace the word or phrase in italics with a key word (or any of its forms) from Lesson 16.

In Shakespeare's *The Tempest*, an evil brother usurps the throne of Prospero, the duke of Milan, and maroons him and his infant daughter Miranda on a deserted island. A (1) *person skilled at summoning spirits by magic*, Prospero soon gains control over the island and its creatures, including Ariel, a fairy-like spirit, and Caliban, a(n) (2) *evil creature without principles.*

When Miranda reaches maturity, however, Prospero realizes this isolated life is not a (3) *substitute* for human society and makes plans to (4) *abolish* his jurisdiction over the island. He magically arranges the shipwreck of a boat carrying his brother and a handsome prince, (5) *acts as a judge* in the case of the sailors who plot with Caliban to (6) *illegally seize* control of the island, and arranges a marriage for Miranda. In the final scene as he departs for his old life he (7) *formally renounces* the practice of conjuration, breaking his wand and "drowning" his magic books in the sea.

1. _____   5. _____

2. _____   6. _____

3. _____   7. _____

4. _____

REVIEW EXERCISES FOR LESSONS 15 AND 16

1 Circle the letter of the best answer.

1. arbitrator : negotiation : :
   a. legate : legislation
   b. surrogate : substitution
   c. exhorter : emergency
   d. conjuror : magic
   e. reprobate : probity
2. vindictive : forgiveness : :
   a. hortatory : domination
   b. surrogate : delegation
   c. perjurious : allegation
   d. censorious : approbation
   e. vengeful : feud
3. adjure : abjure : :
   a. censure : censor
   b. conjure : reprove
   c. arbitrate : adjudicate
   d. arrogate : abrogate
   e. urge solemnly : recant
4. Which root is defined incorrectly?
   a. *rogare* <L. "to rotate"
   b. *censere* <L. "to give an opinion"
   c. *probare* <L. "to prove"
   d. *hortari* <L. "to encourage"
   e. *punire* <L. "to punish"
5. Which word is not derived from *jurare*?
   a. jury   b. judge   c. adjure   d. conjure   e. perjury

2   Matching: On the line at the left, write the letter of the phrase that best
        describes the performer of the acts.

_____ **1.** someone accused of lying   A. a legate with powers of
             under oath   adjudication

_____ **2.** someone criticized for   B. a judicious relegator
             basing decisions on
             personal whim   C. an adjurer to probity

_____ **3.** someone putting false   D. an alleged perjurer
             claims on property without
             getting into trouble   E. a person arrogating with
                                                       impunity
_____ **4.** someone sent on a mission
             to serve as a judge   F. a person reproved for
                                                       arbitrariness
_____ **5.** someone urging others to   G. a person who abjures
             behave with integrity   censoriousness

_____ **6.** someone swearing not to be
             overly critical

_____ **7.** someone wisely dismissing
             something as unimportant

3   Fill in each blank with the most appropriate word from Lessons 15
        and 16. Use a word or any of its forms only once.

In 1999 William Jefferson Clinton became only the second president
of the United States to face impeachment. The charges of

a) _____ (lying under oath) brought against the
president were largely based on information gathered by a special

prosecutor, who had issued a b) _____ (legal
requirement that someone give evidence) forcing the president to

testify. As is its c) _____ (privilege or right), the

Senate d) _____d (acted as a judge for) the
cases, ultimately finding Clinton not guilty.

However history will ultimately assess the impeachment, it had immedi-
ate repercussions. Some people considered Clinton the victim of

a(n) e) _____ (bitter, revengeful feud) on the

part of f) _____ (severely critical) political enemies

and a special prosecutor who had g) _____
(claimed without authority) too much power to himself. As a result,

Congress h) _____d (repealed) the legislation
that had created the office of the special prosecutor by failing to renew
it when it expired. Other people considered Clinton a thorough

i) _____ (mountebank) and in the next

elections demanded greater personal j) _____
(uprightness) in candidates for high office.

4   Writing or Discussion Activities

1. The prerogatives of any person or group are usually jealously
    guarded. Consider a group in your school or community that has
    special prerogatives and describe those in a paragraph. In your
    description illustrate the ways in which these prerogatives are
    exercised. Are special precautions taken to protect these
    prerogatives? If so, describe in another paragraph how these
    privileges are threatened or arrogated and how they are defended.
2. Describe a situation in which someone was censured for some act,
    opinion, or plan and later was vindicated. How did vindication
    come about? Contrast how you or the person felt before and after
    being vindicated.

WORD LIST

(Numbers in parentheses refer to the lesson in which the word appears.)

abate (11)

abjure (16)

abrogate (16)

abstruse (1)

accede (12)

acerbic (8)

acquiesce (1)

acquisitive (7)

acrid (8)

acrimony (8)

acumen (8)

acute (8)

adjudicate (16)

adjure (16)

adumbrate (9)

aesthete (13)

aesthetic (13)

aggregation (3)

allege (15)

altercation (2)

altruism (2)

anarchy (3)

anathema (2)

annunciation (4)

antithesis (2)

apocalypse (10)

apocryphal (10)

apoplexy (10)

apostate (10)

approbation (15)

arbitrary (16)

arbitrate (16)

archaic (3)

archetype (3)

archipelago (3)

archive (3)

arrogate (16)

aver (6)

bas-relief (5)

battery (11)

battlement (11)

beatific (13)

beatitude (13)

bellicose (11)

belligerent (11)

benign (13)

benignant (13)

benison (13)

bona fide (13)

bonanza (13)

bon vivant (13)

boon (13)

cadence (12)

carte blanche (11)

cartel (11)

cartographer (11)

castigate (10)

casuistry (12)

cataclysm (6)

catapult (6)

cede (12)

censorious (15)

censure (15)

chasten (10)

clavier (10)

comportment (8)

compunction (12)

concession (12)

conclave (10)

conducive (10)

conjure (16)

daunt (11)

debase (5)

debonair (13)

decadent (12)

declivity (5)

demagogue (3)

demise (7)

demographer (3)

denigrate (9)

depredation (12)

diadem (10)

diametrical (10)

diaspora (10)

diatribe (10)

dynamo (7)

dynasty (7)

echelon (5)

egregious (3)

elucidate (9)

emendation (14)

emissary (7)

enclave (10)

endemic (3)

ephemeral (2)

epitaph (2)

epithet (2)

epitome (2)

eponymous (2)

eugenics (13)

euphemism (13)

euphony (13)

exacerbate (8)

exegesis (4)

exhort (16)

expunge (12)

extrude (1)

forte (11)

fortitude (11)

gregarious (3)

hegemony (4)

hortatory (16)

hypochondria (6)

hypothesis (6)

icon (3)

iconoclastic (3)

illicit (14)

impeccable (14)

impecunious (8)

imponderable (5)

importune (7)

impugn (11)

impunity (5)

incumbent (6)

indomitable (11)

induce (4)

inquisition (7)

intercede (12)

interloper (1)

internecine (1)

interpolate (1)

interpose (1)

interregnum (1)

judicious (16)

juxtapose (1)

leaven (5)

legate (15)

legerdemain (5)

leverage (5)

levitate (5)

levity (5)

licentious (14)

lucent (9)

lucid (9)

luminary (9)

luminescence (9)

maladroit (14)

malaise (14)

malapropism (14)

malefactor (14)

malevolent (14)

malfeasance (14)

malign (14)

malinger (14)

mendacious (14)

mendicant (14)

meretricious (7)

meritorious (7)

muster (9)

necromancy (9)

obtrude (1)

Occident (12)

occlusion (10)

oligarchy (3)

opportunist (7)

pall (9)

palliate (9)

pallid (9)

pandemic (3)

paradigm (2)

paradox (2)

paragon (2)

parameter (2)

peccadillo (14)

pecuniary (8)

pellucid (9)

penchant (5)

peremptory (8)

peripatetic (2)

peripheral (2)

perjury (16)

plutocrat (8)

politic (4)

polity (4)

ponderous (5)

potentate (4)

predatory (12)

preempt (8)

premise (7)

preponderant (5)

prerogative (16)

presumption (7)

probity (15)

proclivity (5)

propinquity (1)

pugilist (11)

pugnacious (11)

puissant (4)

punctilious (12)

pungent (12)

punitive (15)

purport (8)

querulous (7)

quiescent (1)

rapprochement (1)

recidivism (12)

recluse (10)

recumbent (6)

redemption (8)

redoubt (4)

regalia (4)

regency (4)

relegate (15)

remonstrate (9)

renunciation (4)

reprobate (15)

reproof (15)

requiem (1)

rogue (16)

subjective (6)

sublimate (6)

suborn (6)

subpoena (15)

subsume (7)

subterfuge (6)

succumb (6)

sumptuary (7)

surrogate (16)

technocracy (8)

traduce (4)

transcendent (5)

umbrage (9)

unrequited (1)

vendetta (15)

verisimilitude (6)

verity (6)

viceroy (4)

vindicate (15)

vindictive (15)